FIFTH EDITION

CRIMINAL INVESTIGATION

A METHOD FOR RECONSTRUCTING THE PAST

STUDY GUIDE

JAMES W. OSTERBURG
University of Illinois

RICHARD H. WARD
Sam Houston State University

PREPARED BY LARRY S. MILLER
East Tennessee State Universtiy

LexisNexis®

anderson publishing
A member of the LexisNexis Group

**Criminal Investigation: A Method for Reconstructing the Past, Fifth Edition
STUDY GUIDE**

Copyright © 2000, 2004, 2007
Matthew Bender & Company, Inc., a member of the LexisNexis Group
Newark, NJ

Phone 877-374-2919
Web Site www.lexisnexis.com/anderson/criminaljustice

This Study Guide was designed to be used in conjunction with *Criminal Investigation: A Method for Reconstructing the Past,* Fifth Edition. © 2007 by Matthew Bender & Company, Inc. (ISBN: 978-1-59345-429-6)

Photocopying for distribution is prohibited.

Cover design by Tin Box Studio/Cincinnati, OH

EDITOR Ellen S. Boyne
ACQUISITIONS EDITOR Michael C. Braswell

A Note to the Student

This Study Guide was created to complement *Criminal Investigation: A Method for Reconstructing the Past*, Fifth Edition, by James W. Osterburg and Richard H. Ward. It is not designed to serve as a substitute for the textbook. You will need to read the textbook to fully understand the concepts of criminal investigation as well as to complete the exercises in this Guide.

The best strategy is to look at this Study Guide before reading each chapter of the textbook. Read the Learning Objectives and the Key Terms and Concepts. These will help you focus on important material as you read the text. After reading the chapter in the text, it may be helpful to write out definitions and/or examples for the Key Terms and Concepts listed in this Guide.

A fill-in-the-blank quiz is provided for each chapter, and several chapters have crossword puzzles that test your knowledge of important terms and concepts. In addition, some detailed case scenarios and exercises are provided in the back of this Study Guide. Your instructor may ask you to complete some or all of these exercises to turn in for a grade.

Quiz answers and crossword puzzle solutions can be found in your instructor's *Criminal Investigation: A Method for Reconstructing the Past* Instructor's Guide, which is not available to students.

Contents

Section IV: Special Topics

Chapter 1

The Investigator: Responsibilities and Attributes; Origins and Trends

---

LEARNING OBJECTIVES

1. Define criminal investigation.
2. Describe the responsibilities of the criminal investigator.
3. Identify sources of information at a crime scene.
4. Compare and contrast universal motives to particularized motives.
5. Understand the importance of providing evidence of guilt that is admissible in court.
6. Identify the attributes that are desirable in a criminal investigator.
7. Demonstrate how the desirable traits of mind, personality, attitude, and knowledge help to qualify an individual for investigative work.
8. Appreciate the origins of criminal investigation.
9. Discuss the shift in investigative methods during the early 1900s.
10. Discuss investigative trends resulting from changes in society and technology.

KEY TERMS AND CONCEPTS

Bobbies
Bow Street Runners
comparison microscope
complainant
criminal investigation
cross-examination
eyewitness
jurisdiction
notes
Old Charleys
particularized motive
Peelers
photographs
plea bargaining
rules of evidence
sketches
thief-catchers
third degree
universal motive
victim
Watch of London

CHAPTER OUTLINE

I.   Criminal Investigation Defined

Criminal investigation is defined as "the collection of information and evidence for identifying, apprehending, and convicting suspected offenders." It may also be defined as "the reconstruction of a past event."

II. Responsibilities of the Investigator

A. Determine if a crime has been committed.
   1. The investigator should have an available copy of both the penal law and case law of the state.
   2. The prosecuting attorney may be consulted.
   3. Law enforcement personnel have no authority or responsibility in cases that are determined to be civil in nature.

B. Verify jurisdiction. There is no responsibility for investigations if a crime is not within the jurisdiction of enforcement. However, it may need to be referred to the proper authority.

C. Discover all facts and collect physical evidence. Facts at the crime scene are provided by the victim and/or the complainant and by any eyewitnesses. The investigator should collect any physical evidence or arrange for its collection and examination.

D. Recover stolen property. Reports required of secondhand dealers and pawn shops are of great help. However, accuracy of these reports must be verified.

E. Identify the perpetrator. In addition to identification from records, physical evidence, and eyewitness accounts, the value of motive must be examined.
   1. Universal motive: crimes such as burglary, robbery, rape.
   2. Particularized motive: crimes such as homicide, arson, assault.

F. Locate and apprehend the perpetrator. When a suspect is located, apprehension seldom presents difficulty. However, careful planning and staging of a raid is of utmost importance.

G. Aid the prosecution by providing evidence of guilt that is admissible in court. This necessitates that proper notes, photographs, and sketches are made in a timely fashion from the beginning. All physical evidence collected must be properly handled and examined.

    H.   Testify as a witness in court. Credibility is established when sincerity, knowledge of the facts, and impartiality are projected. The investigator as witness should be familiar with the rules of evidence and the pitfalls of cross-examination.

III. Attributes Desirable in an Investigator

    A.   Abilities and skills.
        1.   The ability, both physically and mentally, to conduct an inquiry.
        2.   Skills necessary to reach the intended objective.

    B. Qualifications of mind, personality, attitude, and knowledge.
        1.   Intelligence and reasoning ability.
        2.   Curiosity and imagination.
        3.   Observation and memory.
        4.   Knowledge of life and people.
        5.   Possession of technical "know-how."
        6.   Perseverance, "stick-to-itiveness," and energy.
        7.   Ability to recognize and control bias and prejudice in one's self and on the job.
        8.   Sensitivity to people's feelings.
        9.   The honesty and courage to withstand temptation and corruption.
      10.   When testifying, not becoming overzealous and not committing perjury.
      11.   Physically fit appearance, report writing skills, good public relations.

IV. Origins of Criminal Investigation

    A.   Historical development—English and French roots.
        1.   Industrial revolution and migration of populations.
        2.   Thief-catchers.
        3.   Jonathan Wild.
        4.   Watch of London—earliest police in England, later known as the "Old Charleys."
        5.   Henry Fielding—Bow Street Runners.
        6.   Metropolitan Police Act of 1829—Sir Robert Peel—Peelers and Bobbies.
        7.   Scotland Yard.
        8.   Francois Eugene Vidocq of France.

    B.   Historical development—United States.
        1.   Thomas Byrnes, New York City.
        2.   Theodore Roosevelt, President of the Board of Police Commissioners.
        3.   Federal investigative agencies, U.S. Treasury, U.S. Department of Justice, U.S. Postal Inspection Service.
        4.   The Bureau of Investigation renamed the Federal Bureau of Investigation under J. Edgar Hoover.

C. Shift in investigative methods.
    1. Wickersham Commission and use of "third degree" by police.
    2. Hans Gross—the father of forensic investigation.
    3. Francis Galton—fingerprint science.
    4. Paul Uhlenhuth—precipitin tests for blood species.
    5. Calvin Goddard—comparison microscope.
    6. Edmond Locard—first police laboratory in Lyon, France.
    7. Paul Kirk—criminalistics.

VI. Trends in Investigation

A. Office of Law Enforcement Assistance (establishment of the LEAA during the 1960s and 1970s).

B. Computerized information systems.

C. Equal Employment Opportunity Act and employment of female investigators.

D. Contributions of research in criminal investigation processes and methods.

Name: _____

QUIZ

1. Criminal investigators have no responsibility in matters that pertain to

   _____.

2. Investigators should carefully document the crime scene by notes, photo-graphs, and _____.

3. Testimony in court is _____ when sincerity, knowledge of the facts, and impartiality are projected.

4. _____ developed the first comparison microscope.

5. In 1931, the Wickersham Commission coined the term _____ when characterizing the methods used by police to extract confessions.

6. The father of forensic investigation is _____.

7. The earliest police in England were known as

   _____.

8. The Federal Bureau of Investigation is housed within the Department of

   _____.

9. The U.S. Secret Service is housed within the Department of

   _____.

10. Francis Galton is famous for his work in _____.

Name: _____

CROSSWORD PUZZLE

CLUES

Across

3   Before the advent of formal police agencies, crime was frequently battled by hirelings known as thief _____.

4   The most significant advance in firearm identification was the development of this microscope by Goddard and others in 1923.

5   London's famous Bobbies were originally called _____. Like the term "Bobbies," the nickname was based on the name of their founder.

9   _____ motives often relate to the victim to the criminal.

12   One of an investigator's chief responsibilities is to gather and preserve physical _____.

14   The earliest police in England worked only at night and were originally know as the _____ of London.

15   Someone who directly observes a crime is called a(n) _____.

Down

1   If a crime is not within an investigator's _____, s/he has no responsibility for its investigation.

2   The _____ Runners were first called "Mr. Fielding's People."

4   The person claiming to have been victimized by a crime is called the _____.

5   Crime scene _____ are used to make an accurate visual record of the scene as the investigator discovered it.

6   During cross _____ by a defense attorney, investigators often refer to their notes made during the investigation to aid their recall.

7   Investigators often make _____ of crime scenes to preserve their observations regarding the physical location of objects at the site.

8   The person harmed by a crime is called the _____.

10   The Wickersham Commission used the term _____ to characterize the extraction of confessions through the use of brute force by police investigators.

11   Members of the Watch of London came to be known as Old _____.

13   Investigators take extensive _____ during an investigation as a means of preserving their observations and reducing the need to rely on the memory alone.

Chapter 2
Physical Evidence:
Development, Interpretation, Investigative Value

LEARNING OBJECTIVES

1. Identify and explain the two major branches of forensic science.
2. Describe the development and interpretation processes of physical evidence.
3. Understand the basic concepts of the details found in physical evidence.
4. Explain the concept of morphological details.
5. Describe how forensic details are developed.
6. Describe the classification process by which an entity is identified.
7. Understand the role of the crime laboratory in reconstructing a crime.
8. Appreciate the investigative value of forensic medicine.
9. Identify the various types of clue materials that can be used as information sources.
10. Comprehend the difference between the natural and environmental sources that produce fingerprints.
11. Describe the means for classifying, identifying, and preserving fingerprint evidence.
12. Appreciate the investigative value of the techniques used in firearms examinations.
13. Understand the significance of semen, other biological material, and DNA profiling in serving the needs of law enforcement.
14. Explain the importance of document examination in developing useful information.

KEY TERMS AND CONCEPTS

associative evidence
Automated Fingerprint Identification System (AFIS)
criminalistics
deoxyribonucleic acid (DNA)
details
fluoresce
forensic medicine
forensic odontology
forensic psychiatry
forensic science
forensic serology
forensics
gas chromatograph
identification

inorganic
latent print
luminescence
mass spectrometer
minute details
morphology
neutron activation analysis (NAA)
organic
paraffin test
pathology
photomacrograph
photomicrograph
record fingerprints
resolution
scanning electron microscope (SEM)
striations
sublimation
superglue procedure
toxicology

CHAPTER OUTLINE

I.   **Forensic Science**

The word *forensic* is derived from the Latin word *forensis*, meaning *forum*. Today, the term *forensics* is applied to or is used in courts of law or public discussion and debate. There are at least two major branches of forensic science—criminalistics and forensic medicine.

A.   Criminalistics disciplines include (but are not limited to):
1. Wet chemistry
2. Instrumental chemistry
3. Firearms and toolmarks
4. Questioned documents
5. Fingerprints
6. Photography
7. Lie detection
8. Voice spectroscopy

B.   Forensic medicine disciplines include (but are not limited to):
1. Pathology
2. Serology
3. Toxicology
4. Odontology
5. Psychiatry

C. Criminalistics is a branch of forensic science concerned with the recording, scientific examination, and interpretation of the minute details to be found in physical evidence.

D. Details in physical evidence.
   1. Fingerprint examples: ridge endings, bifurcations, spur, island ridge, etc.
   2. Firearms and toolmark identification examples: striation markings on bullets or tools.
   3. Other examples of details include DNA coding and chemical trace analyses.

E. Morphology—describes structure and shape (form) in types of evidence. Example would be the jigsaw fitting of glass fragments.

F. Developing details of physical evidence.
   1. Use of contrast (i.e., fingerprint powder, photography).
   2. Use of optical instruments (i.e., camera, microscope).
   3. Use of analytical instruments (i.e., spectrophotometer, neutron activation analysis).
      a. Destructive vs. nondestructive testing.
      b. Organic—contains carbon; Inorganic—does not contain carbon.

G. Identification and identity.
   1. Identification—describes the classification process by which an entity is placed in a pre-defined, limited, or restricted class.
   2. Identity—when the physical evidence is linked to the suspect.
   3. Individual characteristics vs. class characteristics.

H. The role of the crime laboratory.
   1. Help establish elements of a crime.
   2. Link the crime scene or victim to the perpetrator (associative evidence).
   3. Reconstruct how the crime was committed.
      a. Determine if facts are consistent with the story.
      b. Determine time (window of opportunity, time of death, etc.).
   4. Induce an admission or confession.
   5. Protect the innocent.
   6. Provide expert testimony in court.

II. Forensic Medicine: Investigative Value

Forensic medicine is also referred to as legal medicine or medical jurisprudence.

A. Forensic pathology—study of disease or trauma that goes beyond the normal concern with disease to the study of causes of death.

B. Forensic serology—study of blood and body fluids.

    C.   Forensic toxicology—study of poisons (toxins).

    D.   Forensic odontology—study of dental structures and bite marks.

    E.   Forensic psychiatry—study of mental state and probable intent of the criminal.

III. Clue Materials as Information Sources

    A.   Fingerprints.
        1.   Latent fingerprints.
           a.   Natural sources—perspiration.
           b.   Environmental sources—dirt, blood, grease.
        2.   Controlling factors in latent fingerprints.
           a.   Surface.
           b.   Finger pressure.
        3.   Developing latent fingerprints.
           a.   Powders.
           b.   Chemical methods (i.e., iodine, ninhydrin, superglue fuming).
           c.   Radiation methods (i.e., ultraviolet, laser).
        4.   Preserving fingerprint evidence (use of photography).
        5.   Classification and identification of fingerprints.
           a.   Ridge line details.
           b.   Automated Fingerprint Identification System (AFIS).

    B.   Firearms—Questions that can be answered by firearms examiners.
        1.   Matching spent bullets and casings to a particular firearm.
        2.   Distance determination.
        3.   Gunpowder residues.
        4.   Serial number determination.

    C.   Blood.
        1.   Presumptive tests for blood (i.e., tetramethylbenzidine, luminol, leuco-malachite).
        2.   Precipitin tests for species (animal vs. human).
        3.   DNA tests.
        4.   Investigative uses for forensic testing of blood (i.e., locating the crime scene, providing associative evidence, reconstruction of the crime).

    D.   Semen, other biological material, and DNA profiling.
        1.   DNA (deoxyribonucleic acid)—morphology of DNA (adenine, guanine, cytosine, and thymine).
        2.   Types of DNA profiling (restriction fragment length polymorphism, polymerase chain reaction, short tandem repeats).
        3.   Mitochondrial DNA (MtDNA)—passed from mother to child.
        4.   DNA databases—Convicted Offender Index (CODIS).

E.   Document examinations.
    1.   Handwriting and hand-printing.
    2.   Typewriting and machine impressions.
    3.   Paper and ink examinations.

F.   Glass.
    1.   Direction of breaks.
    2.   Bullet holes.

G.   Trace evidence—evidence requiring magnification to establish details.
    1.   Hair and fiber.
    2.   Soil and vegetable matter.

Name: _____

QUIZ

1. The difference between inorganic and organic substances is the presence or absence of _____.

2. Forensic psychiatry is most often employed in _____.

3. Physical evidence that is so small that an examination usually requires magnification is called _____.

4. _____ passes from mother to child only.

5. The study of poisons and their identification by chemical analyses is known as _____.

6. _____ is evidence that links a perpetrator to the victim and/or crime scene.

7. The branch of forensic science that is concerned with the recording, scientific examination, and interpretation of minute details in physical evidence is known as _____.

8. Scratch or machine markings that create individualized characteristics on bullets, casings, and tool marks are called _____.

9. DNA, unlike fingerprints, is the same for _____.

10. Luminol is a _____ for the presence of blood.

Name: _____

CROSSWORD PUZZLE

CLUES

Across

1. The study of poisons.
5. The branch of forensic science concerned with the recording, scientific examination, and interpretation of the minute details to be found in physical evidence.
10. At least two major branches of forensic _____ are recognized: criminalistics and forensic medicine.
11. Forensic _____ is also referred to as medical jurisprudence.
13. A(n) _____ substance is one that contains carbon.
15. The instruments of most significant value for the future would seem to be the gas chromatograph in combination with the mass _____ and the SEM.
16. The scanning _____ microscope (SEM) is a nondestructive instrument for examination of physical evidence.
17. The term _____ is derived from the Latin for "hidden."

Down

2.   When riboflavin and other vitamins in perspiration absorb laser radiation, it yields a visible fingerprint in another wavelength from the incident laser light through the phenomenon of _____.

3.   _____ evidence, a nonlegal term, describes the aspect of laboratory work involving the concept of identity.

4.   The ability of a microscope or camera lens to separate what, to the unaided eye, appears to be one object (or point) into two or more objects (or points).

6.   _____ fingerprints are the exemplars needed by fingerprint experts to identify prints found at the scene of a crime.

7.   The classification process by which an entity is placed in a predefined, limited, or restricted class.

8.   The _____ procedure is a common term used to describe the cyanoacrylate fuming method.

9.   _____ details are occasionally visible to the naked eye but, more often, scientific instrumentation must be used to make them so.

12.   Substances that absorb ultraviolet radiation and instantly re-emit it in the visible region of the spectrum are said to _____.

14.   _____ activation analysis is a nondestructive instrumental method of analysis that is used on inorganic elements.

Chapter 3
Physical Evidence: Discovery, Preservation, Collection, Transmission

LEARNING OBJECTIVES

1. Identify and define the limits of the crime scene.
2. Comprehend the purpose of a crime scene search.
3. Describe the responsibilities of the first officer to arrive at the scene of a crime.
4. Describe the responsibilities of the investigator at the crime scene.
5. Explain the necessity for recording conditions and evidence discovered at the crime scene.
6. Understand the scientific requirements and means of collecting and preserving physical evidence.
7. Appreciate the investigative value of trace evidence.

KEY TERMS AND CONCEPTS

canvassing
chain of custody
coordinate method
crime scene
exemplars
finished sketch
Katz v. United States
Michigan v. Clifford
Michigan v. Tyler
Mincy v. Arizona
res gestae
rough sketch
scale drawing
Thompson v. Louisiana
trace evidence
triangulation method
walk-through

CHAPTER OUTLINE

I.   Defining the Limits of the Crime Scene

The crime scene encompasses all areas over which the actors move during the commission of a crime. Usually it is one readily defined area of limited size, but may be made up of several sites.

A.   Establishing the boundaries of the crime scene.

B.   Pan Am Flight 103 in Lockerbie, Scotland. Largest crime scene search (more than 800 square miles).

II.   The Crime Scene as an Evidence Source

A.   Associative evidence and *in situ* evidence.

B.   *Modus operandi* (method of operation) evidence.

III.   Opportunity for Discovery

A.   *Michigan v. Clifford*—the U.S. Supreme Court reversed a decision due to timeliness of crime scene search.

B.   *Michigan v. Tyler*—requires unnecessary delay in performing a crime scene search without a search warrant.

C.   *Mincey v. Arizona*—requires a search warrant for extended searches.

D.   *Katz v. United States*—the presumption that all warrantless searches are unreasonable.

IV.   Purpose of Search

A.   To locate associative evidence.

B.   To determine the answers to: What happened? How, when, and where did it happen?

C.   Other reasons include establishment of *modus operandi* (MO), establish motive, and identify use or purpose of objects associated with the crime.

V.   Arrival of the First Police Officer

   A.   The first duty is to aid the injured.

   B.   Protection of the crime scene.
      1.   Isolate the scene and limit access.
      2.   Detain and separate witnesses.

   C.   Record information.
      1.   Facts relating to perpetrator relayed to other patrol officers.
      2.   Notes regarding condition, surroundings, and witnesses relayed to investigators.

VI.   Arrival of the Investigator

   A.   Contact with the first officer on the scene.

   B.   Take notes relating to scene details.
      1.   Complainant, victim, time of arrival, time of notification.
      2.   Weather conditions and visibility.
      3.   Witnesses present at the scene.

VII.   Other Sources of Physical Evidence

   A.   Clothing and body of victim (if not at the crime scene).

   B.   The suspect—clothing, weapons, automobiles, house, or other areas under his/her control.

VIII.   Discovery of Physical Evidence

   A.   Overview, walk-through, and search.

   B.   Record conditions and evidence found at the crime scene.
      1. Notes.
      2. Photographs.
         a.   Overall scene.
         b.   Details to establish identity or help reconstruct the crime.
      3. Sketches.
         a.   Rough sketches.
         b.   Finished sketches.
         c.   Scale drawings.
         d.   Computerized crime scene sketch software.
      4. Measurements.
         a.   Coordinate method.
         b.   Triangulation method.

IX. Collection and Preservation of Evidence

A. Preservation—legal requirements.
   1. Identification—an item of evidence must be shown to be identical with that discovered at the crime scene or secured at the time of arrest.
   2. Continuity of possession—chain of custody—evidence must be continuously accounted for from the time of its discovery until it is presented in court.
   3. Vulnerability of evidence—failure to log evidence in a timely fashion.

B. Preservation—scientific requirements.
   1. Deterioration of evidence.
   2. Contamination.

C. Collection of evidence—scientific requirements and means.
   1. Control for variables.
   2. Collection of exemplars and standards.
   3. Sufficient quantities for examination.
   4. Means to collect evidence—tools and containers.

D. Collection of evidence—special considerations.
   1. Trace evidence collection by vacuuming and taping.
   2. Protection from AIDS and other infectious diseases.

E. Transmission of evidence to the crime laboratory.
   1. Follow rules of transporting through parcel post and mail.
   2. In-person delivery is the best means of transmission.

X. Finding Physical Evidence by Canvassing

A. Canvassing to find potential witnesses.

B. Canvassing to find physical and/or documentary evidence.

Name: _____

QUIZ

1. The first responsibility of the first officer on the scene of a crime is to
    _____.

2. Continuously accounting for physical evidence from the time it is collected
    until the time it is produced in court is referred to as
    _____.

3. Sketches of crime scenes compliment photographs in that they depict only
    essential details and _____.

4. Investigators making searches of crime scenes that are not immediate
    should get the property owner's written permission or
    _____.

5. According to the authors, trace evidence can best be collected by vacuuming,
    shaking or sweeping, and _____.

6. Comparison specimens or control samples of known origin are referred to
    _____.

7. _____ is a measurement technique commonly used in
    outdoor crime scenes.

8. The three major methods of recording the crime scene are photographs,
    sketches, and _____.

9. The U.S. Supreme Court case that reversed a decision to allow evidence
    obtained by investigators who entered the scene of a suspected arson five
    hours after the blaze had been extinguished was
    _____.

10. According to the text, the best method to transport evidence to the crime
    laboratory is _____.

Name: _____

CROSSWORD PUZZLE

CLUES

Across

1. In _____ v. *Arizona*, the court held that a warrantless search that lasted for four days was unjustified.
3. Three techniques for discovering _____ evidence are vacuuming, shaking or sweeping, and adhesion to tape.
5. The preliminary _____ process helps to define the boundaries of the crime scene areas to be examined.
6. The _____ method for locating objects at a crime scene is used outdoors.
8. Known comparison specimens.
9. In *Michigan v.* _____, three searches were conducted, but the evidence obtained in the third search was held inadmissible because no search warrant was obtained prior to conducting the search.
10. The _____ sketch, usually prepared later, uses information from the rough sketch, notes, and photographs taken at the crime scene.
11. The _____ scene encompasses all areas over which the victim, criminal, and eyewitness move during the commission of a crime.
14. The process of searching out witnesses who do not know they have useful information about a crime under investigation.

Down

2. The _____ method for locating an object at the crime scene is used indoors.

3. In _____ v. *Louisiana*, the U.S. Supreme Court invalidated a two-hour general search of a homicide scene conducted without a warrant.

4. Any disruption in the chain of _____ may cause evidence to be inadmissible.

7. _____, being an exception to the hearsay rule, may be admitted as evidence for consideration by a jury.

9. In *Michigan v.* _____, the U.S. Supreme Court reversed a decision based on evidence obtained by investigators who entered the scene of a suspected arson five hours after the blaze had been extinguished.

12. The _____ sketch is a relatively crude, freehand representation of all essential information, including measurements, made at the crime scene.

13. A _____ drawing is precise and proportional, with lines drawn by a skilled drafter.

Chapter 4
People as a Source of Information

LEARNING OBJECTIVES

1. Identify the numerous methods of obtaining information from people.
2. Understand the importance of establishing the motive of certain crimes.
3. Understand the importance of an offender's pattern of operation in the identification and apprehension of a perpetrator.
4. Explain the purpose of psychological profiling.
5. Describe the potential importance of evidence brought to the crime scene.
6. Explain the contributions witnesses can make to a criminal investigation.
7. Understand the importance of follow-up activities associated with a criminal investigation.
8. Comprehend how the polygraph can contribute to the investigative process.
9. Appreciate the value of hypnosis in eliciting information from the victims and witnesses of a crime.
10. Explain the investigative value of utilizing voice stress analysis in criminal investigation.
11. Identify the types of nonverbal communication that can contribute to the value of the investigative process.

KEY TERMS AND CONCEPTS

admission
associative evidence
confession
hypnosis
informants
intensive inquiry
interrogation
kinesics
leakage
lineup
modus operandi (MO)
motive
nonverbal communication
olfactory clues
paralinguistics
particularized motive
polygraph
proxemics
psychological profiling

Psychological Stress Evaluator (PSE)
surveillance
voice stress analysis
xylotomist

CHAPTER OUTLINE

I.   The Criminal

A.   Motive.
1.   Universal motive—examples are robbery, rape, burglary. Of little help in furthering investigations.
2.   Particularized motive—examples are homicide, arson, assault. The connection between victim and criminal may be deduced when one is discovered.

B.   *Modus operandi* (MO)—offender's pattern of operation and commission of a crime.
1.   Identification—MO characteristics can identify an offender.
2.   Apprehension—the MO may provide a basis for a plan to apprehend the offender.

C.   Psychological profiling—the psychological assessment of a crime, in which the personality type of the perpetrator is surmised through the recognition and interpretation of visible evidence at the crime scene.
1.   The primary evidence a profiler looks for is psychological motive in crimes in which logical motive may be absent.
2.   Psychological profiling is to establish investigative leads and assist in preparing for interrogation of suspects.
3.   Origin—FBI Behavioral Science Unit.

D.   Clues from evidence brought to crime scene. Physical evidence brought to a crime scene by a criminal may yield a clue to his/her identity.

E.   Confession
1.   Admission—an express or implied statement tending to support a suspect's involvement in a crime but insufficient by itself to prove guilt.
2.   Confessions must be corroborated by other evidence.

II.   The Victim

The victim, like any other witness, is able to provide information that may determine motive and identity of the perpetrator.

III. Witnesses

    A.   The five senses can receive answers to who, what, when, where, and how.
        1. Sight.
        2. Hearing.
        3. Smell.
        4. Touch.
        5. Taste.

    B.   Describing the perpetrator.
        1. Portrait parlé.
        2. Police artists.
        3. Use of Identi-Kit or computer imaging.

    C.   Describing vehicles or weapons.
        1. Vehicles—kind, color, body style, make, model, license plate.
        2. Weapons—kind, color, type, length, caliber, or size.

IV. Persons Acquainted with the Suspect

    A.   Relatives, friends, business associates.

    B.   Use of informants.

V. Follow-Up Activities

    A.   Surveillance.
        1. Locating suspects through surveillance of relatives and close friends.
        2. Determining activities of suspect.
            a. Identify a suspect's associates.
            b. Obtain evidence necessary to establish probable cause for a search warrant or arrest.
            c. Obtain information useful for interrogation of the suspect.

    B.   Lineup (identification parade).

    C.   Neighborhood canvass—seeking information by questioning everyone in neighborhood (intensive inquiry is the British term for canvassing).

    D.   Questioning people: Proposed refinements—old and new.
        1. Difficulties with those who will talk but cannot recall.
        2. Difficulties with those who refuse to talk or withhold information.
        3. Use and value of polygraph examinations.

4. Use and value of voice stress analysis (Psychological Stress Evaluator and Computerized Voice Stress Analysis).
5. Use and value of hypnosis.
6. Use and value of nonverbal communications.
    a. Kinesics—study of the use of body movement and posture to convey meaning (includes eye movement and facial expression).
    b. Paralinguistics—study of the variations in the quality of the voice (pitch, intonation, loudness, softness) and their effect on the meaning conveyed.
    c. Proxemics—study of the physical distance individuals put between themselves and others, noting any shift from an open posture to a protective one.

Name: _____

QUIZ

1. A jury is more likely to be convinced of a defendant's guilt if
    _____ can be established.

2. The most obvious sources of information can be obtained from
    eyewitnesses and _____.

3. A xylotomist is a person who is an expert in _____.

4. According to the text, surveillance is a good method to obtain probable
    cause for an arrest warrant or a(n) _____.

5. A statement that stops short of a written, signed confession, yet admits to
    facts from which guilt might be inferred, is known as a(n)
    _____.

6. Signals emitted in nonverbal communication are known as
    _____.

7. The study of body movements and posture to convey meaning is known as
    _____.

8. According to the text, the principal contribution that the polygraph and
    voice stress analyzers make is _____.

9. The study of variations in the quality of the voice and the meaning
    conveyed by these variations is known as
    _____.

10 The primary psychological evidence a profiler is looking for is
    _____.

Name: _____

CROSSWORD PUZZLE

CLUES

Across

4.   The purpose of a _____ is to have the perpetrator correctly identified by those who witnessed the crime.

6.   Proponents claim the value of _____ stress analysis for the investigator is equal to that of the traditional polygraph.

10. An offender's pattern of operation.

12. A verbal description is also called a _____ parlé.

13. Insight gained during profiling may be useful during _____ by enabling the investigator to induce a feeling of guilt in a suspect that may lead to a confession.

14. A particularized _____ typically yields a connection between victim and criminal.

15. The British use the term _____ inquiry for seeking information by canvass.

Down

1. Nonverbal signals are referred to as _____ by psychologists who study the phenomenon.
2. _____ is the study of the variations in the quality of the voice and the effect these variations have on the meaning conveyed.
3. Psychological assessment of a crime is called _____.
5. _____ pertains to the physical distance people put between tselves and others.
7. A(n) _____ is a statement that stops short of a confession yet admits to facts from which guilt might be inferred.
8. The study of body movement and posture to convey meaning.
9. A mechanical device designed to ascertain whether a subject is telling the truth.
11. _____ may help undo traumatic repression of the conscious memory.

Chapter 5

Records and Files:
Investigative Uses and Sources—
Public and Private

LEARNING OBJECTIVES

1. Identify types of records and files that can be utilized as sources of information for investigations.
2. Understand and appreciate the various types and sources of recorded information.
3. Identify the types of information that can be retrieved from agencies of the federal government.
4. Identify the types of information that can be retrieved from agencies of state and local governments.
5. Identify the types of information that can be retrieved from business organizations.

KEY TERMS AND CONCEPTS

ad hoc agencies
Department of Justice
file-based credit reporting bureaus
investigative credit reporting bureaus
mail cover
mug shot
National Crime Information Center (NCIC)
penal records
police files
probation and parole records
Rogues Gallery
taxonomy
Treasury Department

CHAPTER OUTLINE

I. **Records as Investigative Aids**

   A   Follow-up or provide new leads. Laundry and dry cleaner mark files, fraudulent check files, license plate registration files, pawnbroker files and directories (i.e., telephone, cross-town and city) are good sources.

B.   Identify the perpetrator. Fingerprint files, criminal photograph (mug shot) files, and MO files are useful.

C.   Trace and locate a suspect, criminal, or witness. Most people tend to seek out familiar people and places.

D.   Recover stolen or lost property. Use carefully structured pawnbroker forms and computers.

E.   Ascertain information concerning physical evidence.
    1.   Ownership of evidence.
    2.   The recognition and identification of evidence.

II.   Types and Sources of Record Information

A.   Law enforcement agencies. These files yield the greatest amount of information.
    1.   Police files.
    2.   Penal records.
    3.   Probation and parole records.

B.   Other governmental agencies.
    1.   Federal government.
        a.   Treasury Department (Customs, IRS, Secret Service, BATF).
        b.   Department of Justice (FBI, fingerprint files, NCIC).
        c.   Immigration and Naturalization Service.
        d.   Drug Enforcement Administration.
        e.   Federal Prison System.
        f.   Postal Inspection Service.
        g.   State Department (Passport Agency, Transportation Department, Federal Aviation Administration).
    2.   State and local agencies.
        a.   State agencies (motor vehicle bureaus, labor departments, welfare agencies, *ad hoc* agencies).
        b.   County and municipal agencies (birth certificates, marriage licenses, election records, school records, libraries).
    3.   Business organizations.
        a.   Public utilities.
        b.   Credit reporting agencies.
        c.   Insurance companies.
        d.   Labor unions.
        e.   Fraternal organizations.
    4.   Miscellaneous sources—quasi-official *ad hoc* agencies (i.e., National Auto Theft Bureau, Jeweler's Security Alliance).

Name: _____

QUIZ

1. Most licensing and regulatory powers are exercised through what level(s) of government? _____

2. _____ bureaus gather information on people's lifestyles and reputations.

3. _____ bureaus gather information from creditors and payment records of customers.

4. Information regarding smuggling by use of a boat might be obtained from _____.

5. The _____ maintains records on the manufacture, distribution, purchase, and transfer of firearms.

6. A police file consisting of a fingerprint record and photograph is sometimes referred to as _____.

7. According to the text, files that yield the greatest information for criminal investigations are _____ files.

8. Threatening letter files are maintained by _____.

9. A non–law enforcement agency that maintains records and provides investigations into auto theft is the _____.

10. Miscellaneous record sources, often overlooked, are Chambers of Commerce, Better Business Bureaus, and

    _____.

Name: _____

CROSSWORD PUZZLE

CLUES

Across

1. A common term for the criminal photograph.
7. _____ is a copy of the printing and writing on the outside of a piece of mail.
8. One form of law enforcement files available to investigators is _____ files.
10. The criminal photograph file is sometimes called the _____.
12. The Federal Bureau of Investigation and the National Crime Information Center are agencies of the Department of _____.

Down

2. The U.S. Secret Service, the Internal Revenue Service, the U.S. Customs Service, and the Bureau of Alcohol, Tobacco, Firearms and Explosives are agencies of the _____ Department.

3. A _____ is a classification scheme.

4. _____ credit reporting bureaus gather information on an individual's lifestyle and reputation.

5. The most common, and most comprehensive, law enforcement files available to investigators are _____.

6. _____ credit reporting bureaus collect information from creditors on how bills were paid.

9. The National Crime Information Center (abbrev.).

11 A term for a one-purpose agency is _____ agency.

Chapter 6
Interviews:
Obtaining Information from Witnesses

LEARNING OBJECTIVES

1. Compare and contrast interrogation and interviewing as they pertain to the questioning process.
2. Identify the various methods of acquiring the significant details a complainant or witness may possess.
3. Explain the process that can be used to enhance the identification of stolen property.
4. Discuss the various methods of effectively securing cooperation from reluctant, fearful, or unaware witnesses.
5. Appreciate the purpose of Victim-Witness Assistance Units.
6. Understand the concept and effectiveness of the Behavioral Analysis Interview process.
7. Identify the procedures used during hypnosis.
8. Understand how perception and memory may affect eyewitness reports.
9. Distinguish between the two types of remembering.
10. Identify and explain the four core principles of the cognitive interview technique.

KEY TERMS AND CONCEPTS

artist drawing
Behavioral Analysis Interviews
canvass
cognitive interview
ComPHOTOfit
complainant
complaint report
composite picture
Compu-Sketch
extensive retrieval
eyewitness evidence
fearful witness
focused retrieval
hotline
hypnosis
indifferent complainants
information retrieval

intensive inquiry
interrogation
interviewee
interviewing
investigation report
memory
memory-event similarity
portrait parlé
protective custody
recall
recognition
reluctant witness
sensory input
Stolen/Lost Property Report Form
unaware witness
unconscious transference
Victim/Witness Assistance Program
witness errors
witness-compatible questioning

CHAPTER OUTLINE

I.   Questioning People

A.   Interrogation—the questioning process used for a suspect, or a suspect's family, friends, or associates—those who are likely to withhold information or be deceptive.

B.   Interview—the questioning process used for a victim or eyewitness— those who reasonably can be expected to disclose what they know.

II.   Interviewing

A.   Questions—at minimum, the following questions should be covered in an interview: Who? What? When? Where? How?

B.   *Modus operandi*—an offender's pattern of operation (method of preparing for and committing a crime).

III. Acquiring the Facts

A.   Describing the offender. Several methods or procedures to accomplish a good description of the perpetrator:
1.   Portrait parlé—a verbal description of a perpetrator's physical characteristics and clothing provided by an eyewitness. Loosely translated as *verbal picture*.
2.   Police artist.

3. Pre-drawn facial features (i.e., Identi-Kit, Photo-Fit).
4. Computerized sketch programs (i.e., Compu-Sketch, Com-PHOTOfit).

B. Describing stolen or lost property. Twice described: once by the owner, second by the pawnbroker or secondhand dealer.

C. Taxonomy.
1. Kind of object.
2. Name of manufacturer.
3. Model number.
4. Identifying features.
5. Material used in construction.
6. Physical appearance.

IV. Dealing with the Reluctant, Fearful, or Unaware Witness

A. Securing cooperation.
1. 24-hour "hotlines."
2. Rewards.

B. The reluctant witness.
1. Reasons why potential witnesses are reluctant to come forward.
2. Methods to help convince witnesses to testify in court.

C. The fearful witness.
1. Fear of reprisal.
2. Fear of police.
3. Communication barriers between emergency call takers and complainants.

D. Generating long-term cooperation.
1. Victim-witness units.
2. Use of "hotlines."

E. The unaware witness.
1. Finding unaware witnesses by revisiting the crime scene the following day.
2. Publicizing the crime and broadcasting an appeal.
3. Neighborhood canvass.

V. Indifferent Complainants

A complainant may display indifference or claim that s/he is too busy to be questioned.

VI. Behavioral Analysis Interviews

  A.   The BAI is a technique that seeks to capitalize on the fact that a person being questioned unwittingly emits nonverbal signals.

  B.   Bait questions are sometimes used to draw the individual into modifying or even repudiating the original assertion of noninvolvement.

VII. Hypnosis

  A.   Two concerns:
    1.   In some crimes, the victim suffers severe psychological trauma; reliving the experience through hypnosis could make it worse.
    2.   "Facts" may be implanted to cue or lead the witness under hypnosis.

  B.   FBI policy guidelines on use of hypnosis.
    1.   Training of hypnotist.
    2.   Use of specific techniques to avoid leading the witness.

  C.   Future of hypnosis.

VIII. Eyewitness Evidence: The Role of Perception and Memory

  A.   Stages of observing and recalling.
    1. Sensory input—information is encountered through senses and encoded into memory.
    2. Memory—storage and retention of what was observed and encoded.
    3. Information retrieval—recovery of information through search of memory.
      a.   Recall—to bring a previous event back from memory.
      b.   Recognition—to remember an event after some cue is provided.

IX. Witness Errors

  A.   Environmental conditions—limitations to observing an event.
    1.   Illumination.
    2.   Distance.
    3.   Noise.
    4.   Weather.

  B.   Personal factors—relevant sensory organs other than sight or hearing not impaired in any way.

X.   The Cognitive Interview

A   Memory-event similarity—an attempt to have the witness mentally recreate the environment surrounding the event.

B.   Focused retrieval—the interviewer helps witnesses to focus by refraining from asking too many short-answer, undirected, or irrelevant questions, which tend to break concentration.

C.   Extensive retrieval—the usual mode is to begin at the beginning and continue chronologically to the end. Other means include focusing on the most indelibly inscribed event in memory and proceeding forward or backward, or beginning with how the event ended and working backward.

D.   Witness-compatible questioning—interviewers are better able to ask questions if they can place themselves in the witness's frame of mind.

Name: _____

Quiz

1. _____ is the storage and retention of information that has been observed and encoded.

2. The interpretation, classification, and conversion of sensory stimuli into a more durable configuration for memory is known as _____.

3. One strategy for identifying and apprehending offenders is the collection of a pool of clues from crimes sharing a common

   _____.

4. In the cognitive interview technique, having the witness mentally recreate the environment surrounding an incident is known as

   _____.

5. Although time consuming, the intensive inquiry, or _____, may be undertaken to discover the offender or unaware witnesses.

6. The questioning process that applies to suspects and suspects' family, friends, and associates is called _____.

7. A measure that can be used when a witness fears reprisal should their identity become known to the perpetrator is _____.

8. A fundamental reason why citizens are unwilling to get involved in police matters is the perception that _____ will put them on the defensive and require them to justify their call.

9. A special program that provides counseling and explains each step of the criminal justice process to victims and witnesses is known as

   _____.

10. _____ is a type of remembering in which there is an awareness that something was seen previously.

Name: _____

CROSSWORD PUZZLE

CLUES

Across

1. The _____ Analysis Interview seeks to capitalize on the fact that a person being questioned unwittingly emits nonverbal signals.

5. A _____ requires careful administrative control to ensure that every person in the area is contacted and interviewed.

6. Recognizing and realistically dealing with a legitimate complaint will usually overcome the reticence of a(n) _____ witness.

12. The term unconscious _____ refers to a witness's mistaken recollection about a crime.

14. A fearful witness is sometimes placed in _____ custody to encourage his/her cooperation.

15. Revisiting the crime scene a day or two later, and exactly one week after a crime, may help investigators locate a(n) _____ witness.

16. One method of producing a good description of a perpetrator is to have a(n) _____ draw a likeness of the person observed.

17. The _____ inquiry is Britain's term for canvassing.

Down

2. _____ retrieval employs a variety of methods to encourage witnesses to recall all they may know about a crime.

3. _____ applies to the questioning of a suspect and a suspect's family, friends, or associates.

4. Two kinds of remembering are of interest to an investigator: _____ and recognition.

7. A(n) _____ picture of a perpetrator is made by having a witness choose from a series of pre-drawn facial features.

8. In _____ retrieval, the interviewer refrains from asking too many short-answer, undirected, or irrelevant questions that tend to break the witness's concentration.

9. The person being interviewed.

10. Geiselman and others studied the effectiveness of memory retrieval techniques in a program labeled the _____ Interview.

11. To avoid criticism while retaining the benefits of _____, the FBI has established elaborate guidelines for its use as an investigative tool.

13. _____ is the storage and retention of what was observed and encoded.

Chapter 7

Records and Files:
Nurtured Resource or Arid Archive?

LEARNING OBJECTIVES

1. Identify the major sources of recorded information.
2. Appreciate the investigative value that information science offers to criminal investigation.
3. Understand the principles of crime pattern analysis.
4. Comprehend the importance of identifying crime trends and potential targets through the use of *modus operandi*.
5. Describe the investigative value of utilizing microcomputers to perform crime mapping and to allocate proactive resources.
6. Identify the methods of retrieving various types of recorded information from the records of business organizations.

KEY TERMS AND CONCEPTS

automated data processing
crime mapping
crime pattern analysis
information science
linkage
MAPADS
modus operandi file
proactive resource allocation
ViCAP

CHAPTER OUTLINE

I. **Law Enforcement Records**

    A. Records are set up according to:
        1. Type of offense
        2. Name(s) of offender(s)
        3. Name(s) of victim(s)
        4. Location
        5. Date and time of occurrence
        6. Relevant facts pertaining to the case

B.   Two developments hold promise of enhancing the investigative value of law enforcement records:
1.   Information science—automated data processing systems.
2.   Crime pattern analysis—computers facilitate the greatest extraction of useful investigative information.
   a.   Identifying possible suspects for a particular crime.
   b.   Listing crimes with a common offender.
   c.   Identifying crime trends and potential targets.
   d.   Preparing crime maps by type and location of crime, or by residences of known offenders.

II.   *Modus Operandi*

A.   Linkage—the production of a list of suspects based on *modus operandi* or through crime pattern analysis.

B.   Organization of an MO file
1.   Type of crime.
2.   Time, day, location.
3.   Type of property or persons targeted.
4.   Building.
5.   Object.
6.   Ruse used by perpetrator (represented self as . . .).
7.   Tale used by perpetrator.
8.   Miscellaneous idiosyncrasies.
9.   Photographs.
10.   Electronic data processing.

III.   Microcomputers: Crime Mapping and Proactive Resource Allocation

A.   MAPADS (Microcomputer Assisted Police Analysis and Development System)
1.   Generate special reports and maps locating high criminal activity.
2.   Generate patterns attributable to a particular offender.

B.   Other benefits include managerial proactive measures that can increase police productivity.

IV.   Business Records

A.   Need for cooperation between business and law enforcement.

B.   What records exist and how to find them.
1.   Publications dealing with records.
2.   Directories and encyclopedias.

C.   Access to records and files.
1.   Developing good working relations and contacts.
2.   Keeping the business contact(s) informed of progress.

Name: _____

QUIZ

1. A computer program that produces maps displaying an extensive array of information on crimes within a geographic area is known as

    _____.

2. _____ is the production of a list of suspects based on their MO.

3. The major sources of recorded information are files maintained by government agencies and _____.

4. According to the text, the major difficulty with data processing systems is usually the result of _____.

5. According to the text, crime pattern analysis depends on the sophistication of both _____ and _____.

6. Criminals may not stick to one type of crime, but they generally stick to the same or similar _____.

7. Data for MAPADS are entered daily from the sources of police reports and

    _____.

8. _____ is the collection and analysis of all available information and subsequent circulation of information to operational units within the police department.

9. According to the text, the most obvious basis for division of an MO file is by the _____.

10. One of the disadvantages of obtaining business files is that they are generally_____.

Chapter 8
Informants: Cultivation and Motivation

Learning Objectives

1. Demonstrate an understanding of the legal perspective concerning the use of informants in criminal investigation.
2. Identify the usefulness of information furnished by informants.
3. Describe the different types of informants and their motives for furnishing information to law enforcement personnel.
4. Understand the importance of the relationship between the criminal investigator and the informant.
5. Identify the proper procedures for handling and interviewing informants.
6. Comprehend the legality of evidence based on informant-supplied information.

Key Terms and Concepts

agent provocateur
Aguilar v. Texas
confidential source
contingency funds
Draper v. United States
hearsay evidence
Hoffa v. United States
informants
Maine v. Moulton
probable cause
quid pro quo
Spinelli v. United States

Chapter Outline

I. **A Background on Informants**

    A.   Various names given to those who provide information to authorities.
        1. Sources.
        2. *Agent provocateur.*
        3. Slang terms (i.e., snitch, fink, squealer).

    B.   *Hoffa v. United States*—Court upholds use of paid informants.

C.   *Maine v. Moulton*—court considers inadmissible any incriminating statements made by a defendant to an informant that were prompted by the informant.

II.   Usefulness

A.   Information from informants.
1.   Prevent a crime that is planned but not yet committed.
2.   Uncover a crime that has been committed but has not been discovered or reported.
3.   Identify the perpetrator of a crime.
4.   Locate the perpetrator of a crime or help to locate stolen property.
5.   Exonerate a suspect.
6.   Lower morale among criminal through apprehension.

B.   Types of informants.
1.   Volunteer.
2.   Paid.
3.   Anonymous.

III.   Motives for Informing

A.   Self-serving reasons.
1.   Cutting a deal. *Quid pro quo*—something for something as in making a deal in a plea bargain.
2.   Elimination of competition—usually in vice and narcotics.
3.   Building a line of credit—earn favors from law enforcement or establish legitimacy of business (i.e., pawnbrokers).

B.   Mercenary reasons—paid informants.

C.   Self-aggrandizement—motivated by vanity to provide information, believing it will win favorable attention from authorities.

D.   Emotions.
1.   Fear.
2.   Revenge and jealousy.
3.   Repentance.
4.   Gratitude.

E.   Civic duty.

IV.   Opportunity

A.   Opportunity to acquire useful information.

B.   Opportunity to reveal information without exposure to retaliation.

V.   Cultivation of Informants

Local law enforcement has better opportunity to cultivate informants than federal and even state law enforcement due to opportunities available within a community.

VI.   Dealing with Informants

A.   The investigator-informant relationship.
    1.   Handling informants.
        a.   Meet on neutral ground.
        b.   Treat informant fairly.
        c.   Treat informant courteously.
        d.   Appeal to the reason of motivation.
        e.   Clue in newly recruited informants.
        f.   Explain entrapment.
        g.   Maintain cover.
        h.   Keep informants in line.
        i.   Informants should not commit crimes in return for information.
        j.   Keep financial transactions exact.
    2.   Interviewing informants.
        a.   Press for details.
        b.   Be tactful.
        c.   Check reliability of information.
        d.   Do not reveal discrepancies of information.
        e.   Be sympathetic.
        f.   Avoid embarrassing questions.
        g.   Maintain control of interview.
    3.   Potential problems and precautions.
        a.   Potential for corruption.
        b.   Control of informants by agency or individual investigator.

B.   Similar problems in other fields.
    1.   Newspaper "sources."
    2.   Use of "shield laws."

C.   Problems in other countries.

VII.   Guidelines for the Use of Informants

A.   Guidelines issued by the U.S. Attorney General in 1981 for FBI informants.

B.   Justified use of criminal activity by federal informants.

VIII. Legality of Evidence Based on Informant-Supplied Information

    A.   Probable cause—the most difficult question regarding probable cause arises when the basis for establishing it depends on an unnamed informant's information.

        1. *Draper v. United States.*

        2. *Aguilar v. Texas.*

        3. *Spinelli v. United States.*

    B.   Preservation of confidentiality—reasons for defense attorney to move for disclosure in preparing for trial.

        1. To determine that the informant actually exists.

        2. To determine the reliability of the informant.

        3. To establish differences between the police version of events and the informant's statements.

        4. To endeavor to have the charge dismissed by the court if the state refuses disclosure.

    C.   Cases involving confidentiality.

        1. *Roviaro v. United States.*

        2. *McCray v. Illinois.*

        3. *Smith v. Illinois.*

    D.   Entrapment—occurs when police or informant with official concurrence beguiles an innocent person into committing a crime. Following conditions must be met:

        1. Law enforcement official or a person acting as agent of law enforcement.

        2. Purpose is to institute a criminal prosecution.

        3. Innocent individual is induced.

        4. Conduct constitutes a criminal offense.

        5. Person who otherwise would not do so is prompted to commit an illegal act.

Name: _____

QUIZ

1. The Court reaffirmed in _____ that arrest warrants may be based upon information from informants whose identity is not revealed.

2. _____ is one of the most powerful inducements to becoming an informant.

3. To function as an informant, an individual must have the ability or _____ to acquire information and reveal it without exposure to retaliation.

4. The two primary types of informants are those who are paid for their information and those who _____.

5. Informants motivated by _____ to provide information believe it will win favorable attention from the authorities.

6. This type of informant may betray a rival, particularly in vice and narcotics: _____.

7. The most difficult question regarding _____ arises when the basis for establishing it depends on an unnamed informant's information.

8. Some states have enacted _____ or shield laws, providing varying degrees of privilege in revealing sources.

9. In _____, the Court reaffirmed the "totality of the circumstance" test that traditionally has informed probable cause determinations.

10. The process wherein a defendant agrees to furnish what s/he knows about criminal activities in exchange for a plea bargain arrangement is known as "cutting a deal," getting something for something, or

_____.

Chapter 9
Surveillance: A Fact-Finding Tool—Legality and Practice

KEY TERMS AND CONCEPTS

surveillant
tailgating
technical surveillance
tight surveillance

Chapter Outline

I.   Definition of Terms and Kinds of Surveillance

    A.   Terms.

       1.   Surveillance—the observation of a person, place, or thing, generally (but not necessarily) in an unobtrusive manner.

       2.   Subject—the party under surveillance.

       3.   Surveillant—the person conducting the surveillance.

       4.   Tail—to follow and keep under surveillance.

       5.   Stakeout—surveillant remains in one locale, also known as a *plant* or *fixed surveillance*.

       6.   Undercover—also known as roping, an undercover agent is planted to work alongside the subject.

       7.   Convoy—a countermeasure to detect surveillance.

       8.   Shadow—to follow secretly.

       9.   Be made—to be detected or suspected of being a surveillant.

      10.   Burn the surveillance—when the subject believes s/he is under surveillance.

      11.   Close surveillance—also known as tight surveillance, the risk of being made is great but may be worth the risk.

      12.   Fixed surveillance—same as *stakeout*.

      13.   Moving surveillance—the surveillant moves about in order to follow the subject.

      14.   Loose surveillance—a cautious surveillance also known as *discreet surveillance*; loss of the subject is preferred over possible exposure.

      15.   Open surveillance—little or no attempt to hide the surveillance, also known as *rough surveillance*.

      16.   Mustard plaster—a form of open surveillance in which the subject is followed extremely closely (tantamount to protective custody).

      17.   Plant—see *stakeout* and *undercover*.

      18.   Tailgating—a form of open surveillance in which the subject's vehicle is followed closely.

      19.   Technical surveillance—involves the use of scientific devices to enhance hearing or seeing.

      20.   Bugging—eavesdropping by electronic means.

      21.   Pen register—a device that records all numbers dialed on a telephone.

      22.   Beeper—a battery-operated device that emits a radio signal to a directional finder-receiver. Also known as beacon, transponder, or electronic tracking device.

    B.   Kinds of surveillance.
        1.   Fixed surveillance—the surveillant remains fixed or stationary in one location.
        2.   Moving surveillance—the subject moves about, therefore, the surveillant moves about. Usually conducted from a vehicle.
        3.   Technical surveillance—involves electronic eavesdropping devices and assorted visual and infrared optical devices.

II. The Legality Issue

    A.   Fixed and moving surveillance. The issue of individual privacy and harassment has been invoked to confront these issues.

    B.   Technical surveillance.
        1.   Wiretapping—some states have outlawed all wiretapping, while others permit it to law enforcement personnel with court approval (*Olmstead v. United States*).
        2.   Bugs, pen registers, beepers.
            a.   Monitoring conversations—(*Katz v. United States*)—permissible under the Fourth Amendment so long as there is no reasonable expectation of right to privacy.
            b.   Monitoring telephone usage—pen registers.
            c.   Monitoring movements of vehicles and items of commerce—beepers.
        3.   Electronic Communications Privacy Act of 1986.

    C.   Visual enhancement devices—generally permissible.

III. Practical Considerations

    A.   Tactics.
        1.   Close surveillance.
        2.   Planning.
        3.   Preparation.
            a.   Familiarization.
            b.   Equipment.
            c.   Blending in.

    B.   Discontinuing the surveillance—it is important that the investigator has not been placed on counter-surveillance by the subject.

IV. Procedure for Interception of Wire or Oral Communications

    A.   *Ex parte* orders.
        1.   Probable cause establishment.
        2.   Normal investigative procedures have not been fruitful.

    B.   Time period—normally not longer than 30 days.

Name: _____

QUIZ

1. Generally, federal court cases have considered the _____ Amendment as it applies to surveillance.

2. A countermeasure to determine whether a subject is under surveillance is known as a(n) _____.

3. The party conducting a surveillance is known as a(n) _____.

4. A form of open surveillance in which the subject's vehicle is closely followed is known as _____.

5. The regulation of investigative uses of beepers and pen registers is through the _____.

6. The Court's decision in *Katz v. United States* indicated that the _____ Amendment of the Constitution protects people.

7. A device that records all numbers dialed on a telephone is called a(n) _____.

8. A type of surveillance in which the surveillant stays in one location is called a(n) _____.

9. The party under surveillance is known as the _____.

10. A secret court order in which only one side of the adversarial actors (prosecution or defense) is aware is called a(n) _____ order.

Name: _____

CROSSWORD PUZZLE

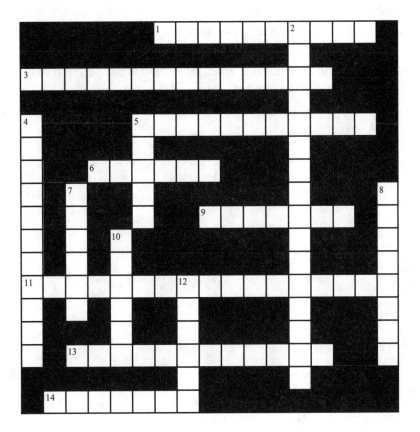

CLUES

Across

1. A(n) _____ agent often gets to know or work alongside the subject.
3. _____ is a form of open surveillance that is tantamount to protective custody.
5. A device that records all numbers dialed on a telephone.
6. Follow secretly.
9. The party under surveillance.
11. _____ is cautious surveillance, and is also termed *discreet surveillance*.
13. The observation of a person, place, or thing, generally in an unobtrusive manner.
14. Eavesdropping by electronic means.

Down

2. _____ is also termed *rough surveillance*.
4. The person conducting the surveillance is the _____.
5. Another term for a stakeout.
7. A countermeasure to detect surveillance.
8. A _____ is also called a plant or fixed surveillance.
10. A battery-operated device that emits radio signals that permit it to be tracked by a directional finder-receiver.
12. A term used to describe an undercover agent getting to know or work alongside a subject.

Chapter 10

Eyewitness Identification:
Guidelines and Procedures

LEARNING OBJECTIVES

1. Describe the procedures for implementing and maintaining an offender's Rogues Gallery file.
2. Appreciate the investigative value of computerized mug photographs.
3. Identify the precautions that must be taken to minimize the chance of misidentification when using the Rogues Gallery file.
4. Understand the guidelines required in using a police artist, as well as composite kits, for creating facial images of suspects.
5. Comprehend the recommendations that apply to investigatory lineups, as well as to lineups held after adversarial judicial proceedings have been initiated.
6. Elaborate on the different viewpoints concerning the reliability of eyewitness identifications.

KEY TERMS AND CONCEPTS

composite images
composite kits
computerized mug photographs
eyewitness identification
file administrator
Identi-Kit
investigatory lineup
jury instructions
lineups
mug shot
Photo-Fit Kit
pictorial identifications
police artist
Rogues Gallery
show-up
sketches

CHAPTER OUTLINE

I.   The Rogues Gallery

A.   Classification schemes.
1.   Mug shot.
2.   *Modus operandi.*
3.   Fingerprints.
4.   Personal description and history.
5.   Type of offense.
6.   File administrator—key to success.

B.   Computerized mug photographs—digital imaging methods.
1.   Edicon Suspect Identification System.
2.   Instant Image Videotalk Workstation.
3.   Compu-Capture.

C.   Using the Rogues Gallery file.
1.   Precautions to be taken to minimize chance of misidentification.
   a.   Random number (6 or more) photographs.
   b.   Police must not give clues to witness.
   c.   One witness at a time for viewing.
   d.   Witnesses must not communicate in any way.
   e.   Once a positive identification is made, lineups should be conducted.
   f.   Make record of all photos shown to witnesses.
2.   Two reasons for making precautions.
   a.   Fair procedure and not open to serious attack by defense.
   b.   Witnesses will testify with greater confidence.

II.   Sketches and Composite Images

A.   Using the police artist.

Witnesses describe the offender and answers questions posed by the artist. The process is repeated until the artist thinks it cannot be improved, or the witness is satisfied.

B.   Using composite kits.

Commercially available kits that offer front-face and profile selections for a wide variety of racial and ethnic origins.
1.   Identi-Kit—uses drawings.
2.   Photo-Fit Kit—uses actual photographs.

III. Lineups

A.   Timing—lineups should be conducted as soon as possible.
   1.   The sooner conducted, the more reliable the eyewitness's testimony.
   2.   Innocent person can be released quickly.
   3.   If suspect is released on bond before lineup, it could delay and/or frustrate the process.

B.   Lineup procedure.
   1.   Composition of the lineup.
       a.   Number and position of participants—varies from state to state.
       b.   Outward appearance of participants (race, sex, physical characteristics, dress).
   2.   Conduct of lineups.
       a.   Suppressing suggestions.
       b.   Recording the procedure.

C   Uncooperative suspects.
   1.   No constitutional right to refuse to be in a lineup.
   2.   Refusal to participate can be used against defendant at trial.
   3.   Can use photographic lineup if suspect continues to refuse.

IV. Right to an Attorney

A.   Pictorial identifications—no constitutional right to be represented by an attorney for photographic lineups.

B.   Lineups.
   1.   Post-indictment stage—Supreme Court held in *United States v. Wade* that suspects had a right to an attorney present but not to refuse to be in a lineup.
   2.   Pre-indictment state—Supreme Court did not extend the right to pre-indictment lineups (*Kirby v. Illinois*).
   3.   Presence of defense attorney at lineup helps ensure that due process standards are met.

C.   Advising the suspect—if suspect has a *Miranda* right to an attorney, they also must be informed they have a right to the presence of an attorney at a lineup.

D.   Waiver of right to attorney. As with *Miranda*, waiver may be oral or in writing, with burden resting on the state to prove is was made knowingly and intelligently.

V.   Role of Suspect's Attorney

A.   Attorney allowed to consult with suspect.

B.   Attorney allowed to make suggestions regarding procedure and observe the conduct of the lineup.

VI.   One-on-One Confrontations (Show-Ups)

A.   Show-up—a one-on-one confrontation wherein a suspect and eyewitness are brought together for identification purposes.

B.   Must be within a short time frame of the offense (within 20 minutes, while some states allow up to two hours).

C.   Use of show-ups when witness is in danger of death.

D.   No right to have attorney present during show-ups but police must not make any suggestion to the witness regarding the guilt of the suspect.

VII.   Reliability of Eyewitness Identifications

A.   Studies indicate that juries overestimate the credibility of eyewitness accounts.

B.   Jury instructions on eyewitness identification.
   1.   Did witness have adequate opportunity to observe the crime?
   2.   Did witness have the capacity to observe the suspect commit the crime?
   3.   Was witness sufficiently attentive to the actions of the suspect?
   4.   Is witness identification completely a result of witness's own memory?

Name: _____

QUIZ

1. Regardless of the classification scheme used in developing a Rogues Gallery file, the primary success of the file depends on the

    _____.

2. If a Rogues Gallery file does not produce results with a witness, the next step is to use a(n) _____.

3. In the absence of forensic evidence, the two most compelling kinds of evidence presented to a jury are a signed confession and

    _____.

4. In *Simmons v. United States*, the Court held that _____ (how many?) photographs were sufficient when using a Rogues Gallery file with a witness.

5. A one-on-one confrontational viewing of a suspect by a witness is called a(n) _____.

6. In a case with damaging eyewitness testimony, the defense may ask the judge to give _____ to the jury to assist them in evaluating the value of the testimony.

7. The Court held in _____ that a defendant had a right to an attorney present at a lineup in post-indictment proceedings.

8. Full-face and profile photographs of offenders are commonly referred to as

    _____.

9. Two of the more common composite kits that are commercially available include: _____ and _____.

10. _____ must be performed as soon as possible, usually within 20 minutes of the crime.

Chapter 11
Interrogation: Purpose and Principles

LEARNING OBJECTIVES

1. Understand and explain the primary purpose of interrogation.
2. Identify and elaborate on the five social-psychological conditions that serve to explain why a person confesses to a crime.
3. Describe the reasons why a guilty person may not acknowledge his/her involvement in a crime.

KEY TERMS AND CONCEPTS

accusation
admission
artificial stimulus
conditional reflex
confession
explicit
implicit
interrogation
natural stimulus
omerta
third degree
Wickersham Commission

CHAPTER OUTLINE

I. **The Purpose of Interrogation**

   A. Establish the innocence of a suspect.

   B. Obtain information from the suspect, relatives, friends.
     1. Names of accomplices.
     2. Facts surrounding the crime.
     3. Follow-up leads.
     4. Locating stolen goods.
     5. Location of physical evidence.

   C. Obtain information from the suspect alone.
     1. Admission.
     2. Confession.

II.   Why People Confess

    A.   Horowitz: Basic concepts.

        1.   Accusation—the person under interrogation must be mentally or visually aware of an accusation.

        2.   Evidence is available—an accusation implies that a certain amount of evidence is available. Should have suspect believe that hard evidence exists.

        3.   Forces—friendly and hostile. Any legally permitted action that either reduces the forces friendly to the accused, or increases the hostile forces, can enhance the likelihood of a confession.

        4.   Guilt feelings—*omerta*—the Mafia code of silence. Most people feel guilt as a consequence of their wrongdoing. Unless they have been involved in gangs with a code of silence, they are likely to confess.

        5.   Confession—the way out. Investigators should make suspects aware that confession is the path to deliverance and mental freedom.

    B.   Pavlov: Basic concepts

        1.   Conditioned reflex—a response to an artificial stimulus or signal can be substituted for a natural stimulus to cause a physiological response.

        2.   Intensity of signal—a signal is received when a suspect realizes that incriminating evidence exists. The stronger the evidence, the stronger the signal.

        3.   Anxiety waiting—to have a suspect wait should produce greater tension in the guilty.

        4.   Alternate signals—a friendly signal may be regarded positively and an unfriendly signal may be regarded negatively.

        5.   Physical condition—an opportunity may present itself to obtain a confession from a suspect when exhausted.

III.   Why Some Do Not Confess

    A.   Lack of conscience.

    B.   Fearful of consequences.

    C.   Some of those who have previously been through the process have learned not to talk.

    D.   Under *Miranda*, it would be unusual for an attorney to fail to advise a client to remain silent.

Name: _____

QUIZ

1. A(n) _____ is an express or implied statement tending to support the suspect's involvement in a crime but insufficient by itself to prove guilt.

2. A(n) _____ is direct and made at the start of the interrogation process.

3. A(n) _____ is implicit and communicated to the suspect by the interrogator's attitude and demeanor.

4. The use of police brutality to extract confessions from suspects is known as _____.

5. According to Pavlovian theory, _____ and other animals react to stress in a somewhat similar fashion.

6. _____ is a term for code of silence.

7. Pavlov found that a(n) _____ could, by repeated association, be substituted for a natural stimulus.

8. Horowitz states that a guilty person's first response to being accused is _____.

9. According to the text, it generally makes it easier for the suspect to confess when their actions are _____.

10 According to the text, greater anxiety and tension is produced in guilty parties by having them _____.

Chapter 12

Interrogation of Suspects and Hostile Witnesses: Guidelines and Procedures

LEARNING OBJECTIVES

1. Understand and appreciate the importance of the *Miranda* doctrine.
2. Identify the procedures that the police must follow to comply with the *Miranda* ruling.
3. Describe the proper procedure for implementing *Miranda* warnings.
4. Identify the factors that lead to the success of an interrogation.
5. Understand the procedures required to conduct an interrogation.
6. Explain the methods of documenting an interrogation and reducing the individual's confession to writing.

KEY TERMS AND CONCEPTS

admission
body language
break
exculpatory
guilt knowledge
interrogation
listening device
Miranda v. Arizona
recording device
subject
Time and Personal Needs Register
two-way mirror
waiver of rights

CHAPTER OUTLINE

I. *Miranda* Guidelines

    A. *Miranda v. Arizona*—doctrine spells out constitutional rights and procedural safeguards.

        1. Right to remain silent.

        2. Anything said can be used against the suspect.

        3. Right to counsel.

        4. Counsel for indigent defendants.

        5.   Wish to remain silent.

        6.   Waiving of rights.

        7.   Admission of statements.

   B.   Congressional action in 1968—issue of unconstitutionality of *Miranda* addressed in 1999.

II.   Implementing the *Miranda* Warnings

   A.   Use of printed cards.

   B.   *Miranda* must be verbally explained and suspect must understand.

III. Waiving One's Rights

   A.   Burden of showing that suspect voluntarily waived rights rests with the state.

   B.   Verbally waiving rights permissible.

   C.   Waiver of Rights forms, signed and witnessed document.

IV. Interrogation in Practice

   A.   Preparation.
        1.   Personally visit the crime scene and/or review crime scene photos.
        2.   Review the entire file and be familiar with details.
        3.   Be aware of physical evidence.
        4.   Learn as much about the suspect as possible.
        5.   Ascertain which elements of crime can be proved by the evidence and which ones cannot.

   B.   The setting.
        1.   Privacy.
        2.   The room.
        3.   Seating arrangements.
        4.   Viewing, listening, and recording devices.
            a.   Two-way mirrors.
            b.   Listening devices (concealed).
            c.   Recording devices.

   C.   Creating the tone.
        1.   Dress and appearance.
        2.   Diction.
        3.   Mannerisms.
        4.   Attitude.
        5.   Taking command of the situation.

D. Conducting the interrogation.
    1. Preliminaries.
        a. Capacity of subject to understand and respond rationally to questions.
        b. Give suspect opportunity to confess.
    2. Beginning the interrogation.
        a. Establish that suspect can remember and is rational.
        b. Questions not related to crime but to general information.
    3. The body of the interrogation.
        a. Establish suspect's whereabouts at time of crime.
        b. Who was suspect with at time of crime?
        c. What was suspect doing at time of crime?
        d. Anyone witness suspect doing any of above at time of crime?
        e. Evaluate responses given (including body language).
        f. The "break."

E. Documenting the interrogation.
    1. Recording confessions.
    2. Types of cases videotaped.
    3. A consensus favoring videotapes.
    4. Reducing the confession to writing.
    5. Witnessing the confession.
    6. Time and Personal Needs Register.

Name: _____

QUIZ

1. The _____ doctrine spells out the constitutional rights and procedural safeguards, including the waiver of those rights, that must be conveyed to the suspect before any interrogation is made.

2. *Miranda* does not forbid statements or confessions that are given
    _____.

3. The conduct of an interrogation is best served if the
    _____ are minimized.

4. According to the text, the most suitable means of demonstrating that an interrogation has been conducted properly and legally is to document the interrogation by _____.

5. The right to have counsel present at the interrogation is fundamental to the protection of the _____ Amendment.

6. According to the text, dry mouth in the suspect, with frequent wetting of lips and asking for water, is a sign that indicates
    _____.

7. Symptoms of lying may be part of the _____ (i.e., that point in the interrogation at which the investigator recognizes that the person is about to confess).

8. Usage of videotaped confessions tends to decline based on the
    _____ of the crime.

9. In order to refute allegations of coercion or duress during an interrogation, an agency might use _____ in the absence of a videotape of the session.

10. The *Miranda* decision reaffirmed and clarified the Court's intention in the case of _____.

Chapter 13
Reconstructing the Past:
Methods, Evidence, Examples

LEARNING OBJECTIVES

1. Understand the concept of the scientific method.
2. Distinguish between the processes of induction and deduction.
3. Explain the differences between classification, synthesis, and analysis.
4. Distinguish between a hypothesis and a theory.
5. Describe the steps that facilitate the reconstructing of the past.
6. Identify and explain the three sources of information needed to reconstruct the past.
7. Appreciate the utilization of innovative applications that can be employed in reconstructing the past.
8. Understand the importance of the investigative mind-set.

KEY TERMS AND CONCEPTS

a priori
a posteriori
analysis
classification
criminalistics
deduction
forensic medicine
hypothesis
induction
investigative mind-set
modus operandi (MO)
physical evidence
scientific method
synthesis
theory

CHAPTER OUTLINE

I. Methods of Inquiry

A. The scientific method.
1. Definitions
   a. Induction—process of reasoning based on a set of experiences or observations from which a conclusion is drawn.
   b. Deduction—process of reasoning that begins with a generalization and moves to a particular fact or consequence.
   c. Classification—systematic arrangement of objects into categories based on shared characteristics.
   d. Synthesis—combining of separate parts.
   e. Analysis—starts with a whole and involves an effort to separate the whole into its parts for individual study.
   f. Hypothesis—conjecture that provisionally accounts for a set of facts.
   g. Theory—a somewhat verified hypothesis, a scheme of thought with assumptions chosen to fit empirical knowledge.
   h. *A priori*—from a known or assumed cause to a necessarily related effect (deductive).
   i. *A posteriori*—denotes reasoning from empirical facts (inductive).
2. Problem identification—first step in reconstructing the past is to identify the problem.

II. Scientific Reasoning Applied to a Criminal Investigation

III. Reconstructing the Past: Sources of Information

A. People.

B. Physical evidence.

C. Records.

D. Innovative applications.
1. Industrial archeology.
2. Garbageology.
3. Theological detective work.

IV. Further Commentary of the Investigative Process

A. Luck or creativity.

B. The prepared mind.

C. A case of unheeded warning flags.

D. Investigative mind-set—more than mere suspicion, it is doubt or mis-givings based on experience that often perceives a connection between two apparently unrelated items.
    1. Watergate.
    2. The Lloyd Miller case.

E. The development of mind-set.
    1. The Vinland Map episode.
    2. The Edgar Smith case.

F. Evidence and proof.
    1. Investigation—art or science?
    2. Art and science as part of a continuum.
    3. Investigation becoming increasingly more scientific.

Name: _____

QUIZ

1. The process of formulating a hypothesis an then looking for evidence to support that hypothesis is _____ reasoning.

2. The process of examining all available information and formulating a hypothesis after the analysis of the information is _____ reasoning.

3. _____ is a way of observing, thinking about, and solving problems objectively and systematically.

4. The systematic arrangement of objects into categories based upon shared traits or characteristics is called

    _____.

5. The process of _____ involves an effort to separate the whole into its parts for individual study.

6. The science of classification is called _____.

7. A deductive reasoning process by which conclusions are reached through reasoning from assumed principles regarded as self-evident is known as _____ reasoning.

8 . An inductive reasoning process by which empirical facts or particulars (acquired through experience or experiment) lead to general principles, or moves from effects to causes is known as _____ reasoning.

9. History and _____ are academic disciplines that reconstruct the past through information from people, physical evidence, and records.

10. _____ is the study of trash in order to determine how a person lives or lived.

Name: _____

CROSSWORD PUZZLE

CLUES

Across

1. The systematic arrangement of objects into categories based on shared traits or characteristics.
4. An object of a material nature that may explain some issue related to a crime.
8. Latin for "from the previous cause."
9. The scientific specialties that undertake most examinations of physical evidence are _____ and criminalistics.
11. _____ starts with the whole, then involves an effort to separate the whole into its constituent parts for individual study.
12. The combining of separate parts or elements.
13. A scientific specialty involved in the examination of physical evidence.

Down

2. A process of reasoning based on a set of experiences or observations from which a conclusion or generalization is drawn.
3. A scheme of thought with assumptions chosen to fit empirical knowledge or observations.
5. A criminal's pattern of operation.
6. A process of reasoning that commences with a generalization or a premise and by means of careful, systematic thinking moves to a particular fact or consequence.
7. A conjecture that provisionally accounts for a set of facts.
10. The creative investigator possesses investigative _____, a way of looking at evidence that enables him/her to discern information about the perpetrator or the way in which a crime was committed.

Chapter 14
What is Crime?

LEARNING OBJECTIVES

1. Distinguish between *malum in se* and *malum prohibitum* types of behavior.
2. Understand the differences between substantive criminal law and procedural criminal law.
3. Comprehend the two components of *corpus delicti*.
4. Explain what is meant by case law.
5. Discuss the purpose of the Model Penal Code.

KEY TERMS AND CONCEPTS

American Law Institute
Bill of Rights
case law
common law
corpus delicti
crime
criminal law
elements of a crime
malum in se
malum prohibitum
Model Penal Code
procedural criminal law
Shepard's Citations
substantive criminal law

CHAPTER OUTLINE

I. Crime

Defined as an act committed or omitted in violation of law forbidding or commanding it, and for which punishment is imposed upon conviction.

A. *Malum in se*—inherently bad behavior (i.e., murder).

B. *Malum prohibitum*—against public policy (i.e., insurance fraud).

C. Perceptions of crime vary over time and across cultures.

    1. Anti-abortion activists may view abortion as *malum in se* while abortion rights proponents may view it as *malum prohibitum* (*Roe v. Wade*, 1973).

    2. Acquiring of wealth; earlier business practices that were legal may now be *malum prohibitum* practices.

II. Criminal Law

A. Substantive criminal law—two classes: felonies and misdemeanors.
    1. Felony—punishable by death or imprisonment for more than one year.
    2. Misdemeanor—punishable by fine and/or imprisonment for less than one year.
    3. Elements of a crime—specific acts taken together compose the crime.
    4. *Corpus delicti*—two components.
       a. That elements of crime be satisfied.
       b. Someone is responsible for the injury or loss sustained.

B. Procedural criminal law.
    1. Based on the federal and state constitutions.
    2. Bill of Rights (Fourth through Ninth Amendments).

III. Case Law

A. Decisions on law interpretation.

B. Prior decisions on interpretation used in present cases.

IV. Model Penal Code

A. American Law Institute proposed a Model Penal Code in 1962 in order to make laws more uniform.

B. Model Penal Code has not been widely accepted by states. (Case law would continue even if the Model Penal Code was universally accepted.)

V. Sources of State Law

A. United States Code and state codes (annotated statutes).

B. *Shepard's Citations*—case law source.

C. Computer online searches.
    1. LexisNexis.™
    2. Westlaw.®

Name: _____

QUIZ

1. The _____ refers to legally binding rules derived from judicial decisions, customs, and traditions.

2. Criminal law that describes forbidden behavior and prescribes the punishment to be inflicted if the law is broken is known as

    _____.

3. Laws that describe the means of arrest and conviction of a suspected offender are known as _____.

4. A person convicted of a(n) _____ may receive imprisonment in jail for less than a year, a fine, or both.

5. A person convicted of a(n) _____ may receive the death penalty or imprisonment for one year or more.

6. The specific acts that, taken together, constitute a crime, are called the

    _____.

7. Previous interpretations and judicial decisions of written laws are referred to as _____.

8. When all elements of an offense are satisfied and a person or person(s) are identified as having committed an offense, the

    _____ has been satisfied.

9. The crime of rape would be considered *malum* _____.

10. The crime of arson to commit fraud would be considered *malum*

    _____.

Chapter 15
Homicide

LEARNING OBJECTIVES

1. Understand and explain the definitions of the different types of homicide.
2. Comprehend the demographic information pertaining to murder in the United States.
3. Explain the investigative activities considered to be normal practice in a homicide investigation.
4. Describe the investigative responsibilities of each person involved in a homicide investigation.
5. Identify and explain the various motives that induce a person to kill another person.
6. Appreciate the investigative value of physical evidence that is recognized, recorded, collected, and preserved in a homicide investigation.
7. Comprehend the fundamental characteristics of gunshot wounds.
8. Describe the primary characteristics of cutting, stabbing, and blunt force wounds.
9. Identify and describe the types of deaths associated with asphyxiation.
10. Appreciate the investigative value of locating people who knew the homicide victim.
11. Explain the investigative importance of written records to the investigation of a homicide.
12. Identify methods commonly used to attempt to cover up a homicide.
13. Explain the fundamental characteristics of incidents involving multiple deaths.
14. Understand the purpose and primary functions of the Violent Criminal Apprehension Program (ViCAP).

KEY TERMS AND CONCEPTS

abrasion
asphyxiation
associative evidence
autoerotic death
autopsy
blunt force wound
contact wound
contusion
corpus delicti
cover-up attempts

criminal homicide
distant discharge wound
dying declaration
evidence technician
excusable homicide
external examination
family abduction
forensic anthropologist
forensic entomology
forensic pathologist
fracture
grounder
hesitation marks
homicide
in-between
incision
internal examination
intrafamily killings
involuntary manslaughter
justifiable homicide
laceration
ligature
"lonely hearts" killer
malice aforethought
manslaughter
mass murder
medicolegal autopsy
murder
mystery
near discharge wound
nonfamily abduction
petechiae
postmortem lividity
premeditation
rigor mortis
runaways
serial murder
suicide
thrownaways
Violent Criminal Apprehension Program (ViCAP)
voluntary manslaughter
wound

CHAPTER OUTLINE

I.   Introduction

A.   Definitions.
1.   Homicide—the killing of one human being by another.
2.   Justifiable homicide—intentional but lawful killing (i.e., execution of a convicted murderer, self-defense).
3.   Excusable homicide—killing by accident without gross negligence and without intent to harm.
4.   Suicide—taking of one's own life.
5.   Criminal homicide—the unlawful taking of a human life.
6.   Murder—the unlawful killing of another with malice aforethought (premeditation); killing during commission of a felony may also constitute murder.
7.   Manslaughter—unlawful killing of another without intent to kill (negligence); may be voluntary or involuntary.

B.   *Corpus delicti*—literally "the body of the crime," it applies to the proof that a crime has been committed. It consists of two components:
1.   That each element of the offense has been satisfied.
2.   That someone is responsible for inflicting the injury.

C.   Demographics.
1.   Of all crime statistics, those on homicide are most reliable.
2.   More than 20,000 murders are reported in the United States each year
3.   Murders occur most frequent in July and December, on weekends or holidays, and at night.
4.   Southern states account for more murders by region.
5.   Male victims outnumber female victims three to one.
6.   Usually, victim and offender are of the same race.
7.   Most victims are in the 20-29–year age range.
8.   There is a prior relationship between victim and offender in about 80 percent of all murders.
9.   Stranger-to-stranger murders are on the increase—decreased clearance rates as motives are difficult to determine.
10.   Most murders are committed with a firearm.

II.   Overview of Investigative Activities

A.   Crime scene.
1.   Record crime scene.
2.   Collect and preserve physical evidence.
3.   Identify the victim.
4.   Establish cause, manner, and time of death.

B.   Ascertain motive for crime.
   1.   Way in which crime was committed.
   2.   Interviews of victim's family and associates.
   3.   Documents.

C   Interviews and interrogation.
   1.   Background investigation on victim.
   2.   Police records.
   3.   Questioning suspects.

III.   Partitioning of Responsibilities

A.   Evidence technician and/or criminalist.
   1.   Records crime scene.
   2.   Collects and preserves physical evidence.

B.   Forensic pathologist.
   1.   Identifies the victim.
   2.   Estimates time of death.
   3.   Establishes the cause and manner of death.

C.   Forensic anthropologist.
   1.   Performs crime scene search.
   2.   Documents physical evidence.
   3.   Identifies the victim.

D.   Detective or investigator.
   1.   Performs crime scene search.
   2.   Ascertains motive for the crime.
   3.   Seeks additional information.
   4.   Questions suspects.

IV.   Motive

A.   Importance—motive provides leads for suspects.

B.   Categorizing motives.
   1.   Financial gain.
   2.   Sexual gratification and/or apparently sex-connected motives.
   3.   Emotional factors.
   4.   Self-protection.
   5.   Interrupted crimes.
   6.   Eliminating an eyewitness.
   7.   Slaying a potential informant.
   8.   Removal of an inconvenience or impediment.

C.   Apparently motiveless crimes.
    1.   Stranger killing stranger.
    2.   Mistaken identity.

D.   Determining motive.
    1.   Crime scene.
    2.   People.
    3.   Records.

V.   **The Crime Scene as the Focus of the Investigation**

A.   Is this an unlawful homicide?
    1.   Establishing *corpus delicti*.
    2.   To be manslaughter or murder, must not be justifiable or excusable.

B.   Is homicide simulated as a suicide?
    1.   Using information from *Final Exit* to stage a suicide.
    2.   Suicide note present.

C.   Who is the deceased?

D.   What was the motive?

E.   Is there associative evidence present?

F.   Reconstructing what happened.

VI. **The Body as the Focus of the Investigation**

A.   Who is the deceased?
    1.   Fingerprints.
    2.   Tattoos and other markings.
    3.   Dental, forensic odontologist.
    4.   Previous injuries, scars, medical procedures.

B.   Establishing the cause and manner of death—the autopsy.
    1.   External examination.
    2.   Internal examination.

C.   Reconstructing the crime.
    1.   Circumstances and where body was found.
    2.   Postmortem lividity (*liver mortis*)—bluish-purple color that develops as blood settles.
    3.   Forensic entomology—insect activity on body.

D.   What time or times are involved?
1.   Last person to see victim alive.
2.   Checking a witness's story.
3.   Time of death.
    a.   *Rigor mortis.*
    b.   Body temperature.
    c.   Other internal factors (i.e., stomach contents, insect growth).
    d.   External factors (i.e., neighbors, residence, personal habits).
4.   Time sequence (time available for killer to commit crime).
    a.   Accuracy of time of death.
    b.   Was there sufficient time to effect injuries?
    c.   Delayed departure (including attempts to cover-up).
    d.   Time line—determining opportunity.

E.   What occurred?—How did it occur?
1.   Autopsy medical terms.
    a.   Abrasion.
    b.   Contusion.
    c.   Fracture.
    d.   Incision.
    e.   Laceration.
    f.   Wound.
    g.   Trauma.
2.   Gunshot wounds.
    a.   Entry wounds—firing distance.
    b.   Characteristics of entrance and exit wounds.
    c.   Number of wounds.
3.   Cutting and stabbing wounds.
    a.   Suicidal wounds (hesitation marks).
    b.   Homicidal wounds (defensive wounds).
4.   Blunt force wounds.
    a.   Blood spatter interpretation.
    b.   Type of weapon used.
5.   Asphyxiation.
    a.   Smothering.
    b.   Strangulation (manual, ligature, hanging).
    c.   Poisoning (carbon monoxide).
    d.   Drowning.
6.   Burns.
    a.   Are the remains human?
    b.   Was the victim dead or alive when the fire started?
    c.   Use of fire to cover up a homicide.
    d.   Antemortem and postmortem injuries.

VII. **People: Those Who Knew the Victim**

A. Canvassing.

B. Informants.

C. Questioning suspects.

VIII. **The Value of Records in Homicide Investigation**

A. Insight into motive.
1. Who benefits?
2. Diaries and letters.

B. Tracing ownership.
1. Firearms.
2. Prescriptions (i.e., eyeglasses).
3. Vehicles.

C. Previously recorded activities.
1. Bills, loans, and credit problems.
2. Bank accounts.
3. Employment history.
4. Insurance policies, wills.

IX. **Types of Homicide Investigations**

A. Definitions.
1. Homicide investigation categories: grounders, mysteries, in-betweens, red balls.
   a. Grounder—case that is easily solved (also known as *platter*, *dunker*, *meatball*).
   b. Mystery—(who-done-it case)—no apparent solution.
   c. In-between—homicide that appears to have a solution but will require effort.
   d   Red ball—major investigation that has the community agitated.

X. **Cover-Up Attempts**

A. Accidental means—make death appear accidental.
1. Vehicles.
2. Firearms.
3. Fire.
4. Poison.

B.   Explainable means.
1.   Simulated felony.
2.   Self-defense.

C.   Diversionary means—to deceive investigator.
1.   First person to report the crime.
2.   Contrived alibi.
3.   Ruse.
4.   Partial cover-ups—more likely when crime is not premeditated.

XI.   Missing Persons

A.   Apparently involuntary disappearances.
1.   Children.
   a.   Family abduction—when a family member abducts a child.
   b.   Non-family abduction—coerced and unauthorized taking of a child.
   c.   Runaways—children who have left home without permission.
   d.   Thrownaways—children who have been told to leave the household
   e.   Lost, injured, otherwise missing.
2.   Adults.
3.   Adolescents.

B.   Misleading reports.

XII.   Multiple Deaths

A.   Distinctions.
1.   Serial killing.
2.   Mass murder.

B.   Several mortalities—all part of one event.
1.   Double homicide.
2.   Family/residence murders.
   a.   Intrafamily killings—guilty party most likely to be an adolescent son.
   b.   Home and workplace invasions.
3.   Mass murders.
   a.   Random shootings—all victims die in one event.

C.   Multiple killings—separate events spread over time.
   1. Crime-spree murders.
   2. Serial murders—usually prompted in males with a sexual drive to exert power through killing.
      a.   Use of ViCAP.
      b.   Role of routine police work.
3. "Lonely hearts" killings.
4. Poisonings.

XIII. Miscellaneous Concerns

A.   Dying declarations.
   1. Victim must believe s/he is about to die.
   2. The victim must have no hope of recovery.
   3. Declaration must identify the person responsible, state the circumstances and manner by which the injuries were sustained.
   4. Victim must be rational and competent.
   5. Victim must die from the injuries received.

B.   Investigator and forensic pathologist determine whether victim was rational and did die from the injuries. Investigator must ask questions regarding whether victim believes s/he is about to die.

Name: _____

QUIZ

1. Homicide involving the intentional, yet lawful, killing of another person is known as _____.

2. Homicide involving the accidental killing of another person, without gross negligence and without the intent to injure, is known as

   _____.

3. The two types of clue materials most frequently involved in the reconstruction of a homicide are _____ and

   _____ evidence.

4. The medical term for the bluish-purplish color that develops as a result of blood settling in the body is known as

   _____.

5. _____ is the medical term for bodily injuries produced by sudden physical force.

6. The tearing of tissue surrounding a gunshot wound is indicative of the muzzle of the gun being _____.

7. _____ is the term used for short, superficial cut wounds inflicted before a fatal wound in suicides.

8. _____ deaths are those that occur when an individual, usually a young male, engages in solitary sex-related activity whereby he is asphyxiated accidentally.

9. According to the text, a(n) _____ is more likely to be the guilty party in intrafamily killings.

10. One of the indications of strangulation is _____ in the eyes of the deceased.

Name: _____

CROSSWORD PUZZLE

CLUES

Across

5. Postmortem _____ is the medical term describing the bluish-purple color that develops after death in the undermost parts of the body.

6. The killing of a human being by accident without gross negligence and without intent to injure is called _____ homicide.

8. A(n) _____ discharge wound results from firing a handgun at a distance of six to 24 inches, or a rifle at a distance of six to 36 inches.

10. The intentional but lawful killing of another human being is called _____ homicide.

12. A case that is easily solved.

13. A(n) _____ wound results when a small weapon is fired while in contact with the skin.

14. The stiffening of the body after death.

15. _____ death occurs when an individual engages in a solitary, sex-related activity whereby s/he is accidently asphyxiated.

Down

1. Wounds that are a product of neither a penetrating nor a cutting instrument.
2. _____ marks are typically seen on the neck of a victim of strangulation or hanging.
3. _____ marks typify suicide and suicide attempts.
4. A superficial, scraped surface area of tissue produced by friction.
7. The forensic _____ is responsible for identifying the victim, estimating the time of death, and establishing the cause and manner of death.
9. A hemorrhage beneath the skin; a bruise.
11. A sign of strangulation consisting of pinhead-sized red dots that are minute hemorrhages.

Chapter 16
Robbery

LEARNING OBJECTIVES

1. Identify and describe the sociological and demographic variables associated with robbery.
2. Understand and be familiar with the definitions of theft and other related offenses.
3. Identify and discuss the characteristics of the robbery suspect.
4. Describe the proper procedures for conducting a criminal investigation of a robbery.
5. Identify and explain the specific types of physical evidence that should be considered by the investigator at the scene of a robbery.
6. Appreciate the usefulness of records and other sources of information that can assist an investigation of robbery.

KEY TERMS AND CONCEPTS

armed robbery
computer imaging systems
crime pattern analysis
Model Penal Code
National Crime Victimization Survey (NCVS)
opportunist robber
professional robber
robbery
strong-arm robbery
U.S. Bureau of Justice Statistics

CHAPTER OUTLINE

I.   Introduction

    A.   Statistics
        1. In 90 percent of robberies, the suspect is a male.
        2. Most robberies occur in metropolitan areas.
        3. Most robberies are committed by strangers.
        4. Sixty percent of robberies occur in the evening.
        5. Offenders displayed a weapon in about half of all robberies.

B.   Definitions.
1.   Model Penal Code definition: A person is guilty of robbery if, in the course of committing a theft, s/he:
a.   Inflicts serious bodily harm upon another; or
b.   Threatens another with or purposely puts another in fear or serious bodily injury; or
c.   Commits or threatens to commit any felony of the first or second degree.
2.   Robbery is generally defined as the unlawful taking or attempted taking of property that is in the immediate possession of another, by force or threat of force.

II.   People

A.   Victims and witnesses.
1.   Males are victimized more than twice as often as females.
2.   Persons ages 12-24 have a higher probability of being a victim.
3.   Blacks are victimized three times more than whites, Hispanics twice as often as whites.
4.   People making less than $7,500 are victimized more than three times as much as those making more than $35,000.
5.   Most people do not make good witnesses because it happens so quickly and there is a high degree of stress.

B.   Types of robberies.
1.   Street robberies.
2.   Residential robberies.
3.   Bank and armored car robberies.
4.   Commercial robberies.

C.   Categories.
1.   Armed robbery—involves the use of a weapon or threat of the use of a weapon.
2.   Strong-arm robbery—involves the use of physical force or the threat of physical force.

D.   Suspects.
1.   Average age of robbers is under 25.
2.   Blacks and males are overrepresented.
3.   Most robberies involve more than one offender on a single victim.
4.   Older offenders are more likely to plan the act.
5.   Younger offenders are more likely to act in groups.

III. Conducting the Investigation

    A.   Physical evidence.
        1. Footprints, fingerprints, and other associative evidence.
        2. Saliva (on face masks), blood, and other body fluids.

    B.   Records and other sources of information.
        1. Robbery suspects usually have prior arrest records.
        2. Most robbery suspects will commit more than one robbery—link crimes together for a more accurate profile.
        3. Police and court records.
        4. Social service agencies (unemployment offices, housing offices, drug rehabilitation programs).
        5. Credit card companies (particularly if cards were taken during robbery).
        6. Motor vehicle bureau records.
        7. Other sources of information (other investigators, patrol information, informants, stores where weapons are purchased, closed-circuit television tapes recovered from scene).

IV. Follow-Up Activities

Successful investigation depends on ability of the investigator to recognize variables, patterns, geographic locations, types of victims, and characteristics of suspects.

Name: _____

QUIZ

1. Statistics indicate that robbers who use _____ as weapons have a higher probability of carrying out a robbery than those using other types of weapons.

2. The use of a weapon, such as a knife or gun, to commit a robbery is known as _____.

3. The threat of using physical force in order to rob is known as _____.

4. Well-planned robberies are usually the result of _____ (what age group?) robbers.

5. Younger robbers usually commit robberies in _____ against a single victim.

6. Robbers usually have _____ arrest records.

7. In terms of geographic location, most robberies take place in _____ regions.

8. According to the text, robbery is considered a _____ crime, thereby placing the victim in a position to be an eyewitness to the crime.

9. It is risky for investigators to rely solely on _____, rather than have corroborating physical evidence to back it up.

10. Blacks are _____ times more likely to be victims of robbery than whites, and Hispanics are _____ times more likely to be victims of robbery than whites.

Chapter 17
Rape and Other Sex Crimes

LEARNING OBJECTIVES

1. Understand the definitions and elements of the various types of sex-related offenses.
2. Identify the two aspects of sex crime investigations that must receive priority handling.
3. Comprehend the proper procedures for conducting follow-up interviews with rape victims, witnesses, and offenders.
4. Describe the proper techniques for conducting a criminal investigation of sex-related offenses.
5. Appreciate the usefulness of records and other sources of information in sex-related investigations.
6. Understand the importance of rape offender profiles.
7. Identify the follow-up activities an investigator should perform as a routine practice in sex-related crimes.

KEY TERMS AND CONCEPTS

anal swabbings
catch paper/cloth
child rape
computerized graphics
consent
crime analysis unit
date rape
deoxyribonucleic acid (DNA)
elderly rape
fingernail scrapings
follow-up interview
forcible rape
gang rape
head hair combing
nasal mucous sample
oral rinse
oral swabbings
penile swabbings
pubic hair combing
rape
rape offender profile
sodomy

spermatozoa
target of opportunity
vaginal aspirate
vaginal swabbings

CHAPTER OUTLINE

I.   Introduction

A large percentage of rapes are never reported. Divorced and separated females are more frequently victimized than those never married. Victimization is higher in metropolitan areas. About one-half of victims are under the age of 18. In more than one-half of the cases, the rapist and the victim are acquainted or know each other.

A.   Definitions—legal definitions of rape generally involve the following elements:
1.   Sexual penetration of the victim's vulva;
2.   By a person or persons without victim's consent;
3.   Or with a minor child.

B.   Other forms of sex-related crimes include:
1.   Sexual assault
2.   Child abuse and molestation (pedophilia)
3.   Some forms of pornography
4.   Indecent exposure
5.   Incest
6.   Stalking

II.   Stalking

A.   Typologies.
1.   Psychopathic Personality Stalker—usually a male from a dysfunctional family who is likely to use violence as a form of control over a former girlfriend or wife. Most common form of stalker.
2.   Psychotic Personality Stalker—male or female who becomes obsessed with a particular person.
3.   Celebrity Stalker—person who follows someone who is famous, usually entertainment or sports figures.
4.   Lust Stalker—involves desire for sexual (rape) gratification or psychological gain or power over a stranger.
5.   "Hit Man" Stalker—professional killer who stalks victims.
6.   Love-Scorned Stalker—involves prior personal relationship between stalker and victim.
7.   Domestic Stalker—involves anger against a spouse.
8.   Political Stalker—focuses on a political figure, usually not personally known by the stalker.

B. Propensity for violence.
   1. Most stalkers do not intend to murder their victims (an exception is the "love-scorned stalker").
   2. All stalkers have a propensity for violence that may result in murder.

III. People

A. Two priorities for law enforcement. Attitude and demeanor of investigator is crucial during the initial stages of investigation if these two priorities are to be accomplished successfully.
   1. Seeing that victim receives proper medical attention.
   2. Protection of the crime scene and collection of evidence.

B. Victims and witnesses.
   1. Goals of preliminary interview.
      a. Obtain physical description of offender(s).
      b. Determine location where crime took place.
      c. Identify possible witnesses.
      d. Determine specific actions of the offender volunteered by the victim.
      e. Determine circumstances leading to attack.
      f. Obtain information on weapons and vehicles used.
      g. Determine specific location of attack
   2. Interviews of victim should never be conducted in front of husbands, boyfriends, or other family members.
   3. Victim assistance counselors or psychologists are of great assistance to victims and family members.

IV. Follow-Up Interviews

A. Conduct of the interview.
   1. Avoid use of the police station.
   2. Use counselors for support if established by departmental policy.
   3. Be careful not to "lead" the victim or witness in telling the story.
   4. Allow victim/witness to use own terminology for describing parts of body, sexual acts, etc.
   5. Obtain exact phrases or words used by the offender (helps to establish MO).

B. Establish elements of the crime through interview.
   1. Forcible rape.
   2. Consent.
   3. Date rape.

C.   Interviewing children.
1.   Interviews should be conducted with the assistance of trained professionals (i.e., child protective services workers).
2.   States have varying degrees of legal guidelines in police and social worker intervention in abused and molested children cases.

V.   Conducting the Investigation

A.   Physical evidence.
1.   Sex crimes investigation kits—designed to collect evidence by medical personnel.
2.   Crime scene search should locate and preserve evidence that:
a.   Links the victim and the offender to the crime scene.
b.   Establishes that sexual relations took place.
c.   Establishes that force was used.
d.   Establishes the offender's role or activity.
3.   DNA evidence.
4.   Types of physical evidence.
a.   Clothing (victim and offender).
b.   Head hair combings (victim and offender).
c.   Known head hair samples (victim and offender).
d.   Pubic hair combings (victim and offender).
e.   Known pubic hair samples (victim and offender).
f.   Vaginal swabbings.
g.   Oral swabbings.
h.   Anal swabbings.
i.   Microscope slides of smears from swabbings.
j.   Penile swabbings.
k.   Vaginal aspirate (vaginal vault irrigation).
l.   Oral rinse.
m.   Nasal mucous sample.
n.   Fingernail scrapings (clippings).
o.   Debris collection (on body, clothing, etc.).
p.   Known blood sample (victim and offender).
q.   Known saliva sample (victim and offender to assist in determining if secretors).
r.   "Catch paper/cloth" (victim stands on while undressing to catch any debris that may be of evidential value).

B.   Records and other sources of information.
1.   Prior arrests (determine if a "target of opportunity" offense).
2.   *Modus operandi.*
3.   Sex offender lists (i.e., child molesters).

C.   Profiling offenders.
    1. ViCAP.
    2. Patterns of rapes.
        a.   Gang rape.
        b.   Elderly rape.
        c.   Child rape.
        d.   Serial rapists.

VI. Follow-Up Activities

While the primary duty of the investigator is to prepare a case for prosecution, the emotion of the situation may interfere with the investigation. It is vitally important that the investigator use sympathy and an understanding demeanor when conducting the investigation.

Name: _____

QUIZ

1. One of the most important requirements in interviewing victims of sexual assault is to be _____ with the victim.

2. Most rape victims are under the age of _____.

3. Care must be taken to determine the _____ of the victim because consent is a common defense against rape.

4. Interviews of child victims of rape should be made with the assistance of _____.

5. The recovery of weapons or materials used to restrain the victim at the crime scene helps establish that _____ was used in the attack.

6. Collection of physical evidence from the victim (i.e., vaginal swabbings, etc.) should be performed by a(n) _____.

7. The use of a(n) _____ is based on the theory that an individual displays unique characteristics in personality, crime scene behavior, and MO.

8. The most common form of stalker is the _____.

9. The type of stalker that becomes obsessed with a particular person, such as an unobtainable love subject, is the _____.

10. In a study of serial rapists, a large majority had been _____ as children.

Chapter 18
Burglary

LEARNING OBJECTIVES

1. Identify and explain the various types of burglary that are typical in the United States.
2. Describe the primary characteristics of burglary offenses.
3. Identify the demographic characteristics of the burglary victim.
4. Understand the Model Penal Code's definition of burglary.
5. Identify the more common techniques used by burglars to gain entry into a building or residence.
6. Describe the proper procedures for conducting a criminal investigation of burglary.
7. Appreciate the importance of collecting and preserving physical evidence found at the scene of a burglary.
8. Understand the investigative usefulness of records and other sources of information that may link stolen property to a crime scene.

KEY TERMS AND CONCEPTS

alarm bypass
beeping
burglary
career burglar
case screening
casing
cat burglar
cutting glass
cutting wall
easy mark
fence
fishing
juvenile offender
lock-in
loiding
National Auto Theft Bureau (NATB)
National Crime Information Center (NCIC)
partying
picking
prying
pulling
second-story job

slap hammer
slipping lock
skylight entry
smash and crash
solvability factors
strings
transom entry

CHAPTER OUTLINE

I.   Introduction

A.   Statistics.
1.   It is estimated that more than 70 percent of all households will be burglarized at least once over a 20-year period.
2.   Probability of victimization is higher for central-city homes and homes headed by young blacks.
3.   Estimated that almost one-half of all burglaries are reported to police.
4 .   Preliminary analysis of burglary cases can produce "solvability factors" that make it possible to focus on those cases with the highest probability of being solved.

B.   Definitions.
1.   The Model Penal Code offers the following:

A person is guilty of burglary if s/he enters a building or occupied structure, or separately secured or occupied portion thereof, with purpose to commit a crime therein, unless the premises are at the time open to the public or the actor is licensed or privileged to enter. It is an affirmative defense to prosecution for burglary that the building or structure was abandoned.

2.   The *Bureau of Justice Statistics Dictionary* defines burglary as:

Unlawful entry of any fixed structure, vehicle, or vessel used for regular residence, industry or business, with or without force, with the intent to commit a felony or larceny.

II. People

A. Victims.
1.   Understanding the type of burglary, the characteristics of the offense, and the demographic characteristics of the victim can provide insight into the suspect and his/her background (i.e., more experienced burglars will unlock all doors and windows in a residence to exit quickly in case the owner returns).

2. Questions that might produce useful information:
   a. Anything unique about the timing of the burglary.
   b. Prior attempts or successful burglaries.
   c. Who knew property and location.
   d. Is property unique, including items such as art objects?
   e. Have there been similar burglaries?
   f. Any publicity in newspapers (i.e., wedding announcements)?
3. The public.
   a. Possible witnesses include neighbors, mail carriers, delivery persons, utility meter readers, and telephone company workers.
   b. Petty criminals known in neighborhood could be a source of information.
4. The burglary suspect.
   a. Common techniques to gain entry (i.e., prying, smash and crash, loiding).
   b. MO may be recognized by looking at techniques used to gain entry.

III. Conducting the Investigation

A. Repetition is a predominant characteristic of burglary. Burglaries are generally committed repeatedly using the same or similar technique until the suspect is caught.

B. Physical evidence.
   1. Fingerprints—most common form of physical evidence at the crime scene.
   2. Trace evidence—such as blood, saliva, footprints, hair, fibers, cigarettes, matchbooks, tools, clothing, handwriting.
   3. Areas to be searched include: garbage can, items in refrigerator, toilet seat, locks, documents.

C. Records and other sources of information.
   1. NCIC.
   2. NATB.
   3. Credit card companies.
   4. Chambers of commerce (in crimes against businesses).
   5. Strings—groups of characters used in computer searches, helpful in looking for records of stolen property with no serial numbers recorded or affixed to property.

IV. Follow-Up Activities

    A. Burglary investigation involves several stages:
        1. Investigating crime scene.
        2. Interviewing witnesses.
        3. Using informants.
        4. Examining records.
        5. Tracing property.
        6. Identifying suspects.

    B. Most burglars are known to the police because they have prior records and a large number are drug users.

Name: _____

QUIZ

1. Burglary is a seasonal crime, with more occurring during the
   _____ months.

2. Burglaries of middle-class or poor residences are more likely to be
   committed by _____.

3. The use of a jimmy, screwdriver, tire iron, pry bar, or knife to gain entry
   through a door or window is known as

   _____.

4. Slipping a lock or _____ is an entry technique that
   uses a credit card or knife slipped between the lock and the door jamb.

5. _____ make it possible to focus
   only on those cases with the highest probability of clearance by arrest.

6. The _____ not only
   provides information on stolen vehicles, but also on property taken from
   trucks.

7. The most common form of physical evidence found at a crime scene is/are

   _____.

8. The use of _____ for computer searches of data-
   bases of stolen property allows for easier searching of records of stolen
   property with no serial numbers.

9. A(n) _____ is a burglar that enters homes while
   residents are present, usually at night.

10 Between business establishments and residential homes, the vast majority
   of burglaries are _____ (what kind?).

Name: _____

CROSSWORD PUZZLE

CLUES

Across

2. _____ a garage door involves using an electronic opener on the correct frequency to open the door while the owner is out.
3. Burglars often dispose of the items they steal by selling them to a _____.
5. Using a knife or professional locksmith's pick to open the cylinder of a lock.
7. Using a credit card, knife, or other slim material to slip between a lock and a doorjamb where there is no deadbolt or other latch.
8. Cutting _____ involves the use of a suction cup, such as a toy dart, to keep the cut material from falling.
11. A _____ entry involves breaking or removing the air conditioner and climbing in through the transom.
13. _____ factors are used to screen cases to identify those with the highest probability of solution.
14. Using a jimmy, screwdriver, or other such tool to force a door, window, or lock.
15. According to the text, a theft need not be committed to establish a charge of _____.
16. The National Auto Theft Bureau (abbreviation).
17. Using an auto body repair tool called a "slap hammer" to pull a lock cylinder out.

Down

1. A(n) _____ entry involves lowering oneself through a window on the roof of a building.
2. An alarm _____ involves neutralizing an alarm system.
3. Breaking a hole in a window and reaching in by hand or with a pole to remove items.
4. Many burglars operate with very little planning or _____ of the target and the victim.
6. Slap _____ is another name for an auto body dent repair tool used to pull a lock cylinder.
7. Entering a facility before closing and hiding in the premises until after closing.
9. A(n) _____ job involves gaining entry to a structure through upper floor windows or the roof.
10. Entering a residence where a barbecue, pool, or interior party is being held and stealing loose items.
12. Another term for loiding.

Chapter 19
Arson

1. Identify and explain the elements of the crime of arson.
2. Appreciate the usefulness of various types of people as sources of information to an arson investigation.
3. Describe the proper procedure for a criminal investigation of arson.
4. Understand the purpose of examining the fire scene and the need for collection and preservation of physical evidence.
5. Comprehend the significance of locating the fire's point of origin and the sources of its ignition.
6. Identify the various types of motives that precipitate the crime of arson.
7. Appreciate the investigative usefulness of recorded evidence that may exist to support a motive for arson.

KEY TERMS AND CONCEPTS

accelerant
alligatoring
arson
burn patterns
carbon dioxide
carbon monoxide
catalytic combustion/resistance analysis
charring
combustion
crazing
flame ionization
flashover
fuel
gas chromatography
heat distortion
incendiary
ignition
infrared spectrophotometry
organic compounds
oxidation
oxygen
phosphorus
plant

point of origin
pour patterns
pyromania
sniffer
spalling
spontaneous combustion
straw ownership
streamers
trailer
"V" pattern

CHAPTER OUTLINE

I.   Introduction

    A.   Statistics.
        1.   An estimated 3 to 6 percent of all structural fires in the United States are intentionally set or suspicious.
        2.   20 percent of arson cases result in an arrest.
        3.   Almost one-half (46%) of arson perpetrators are juveniles.
        4.   Difficult to investigate and obtain evidence.
            a.   Fire may consume all traces of its incendiary origin.
            b.   Crime scene may be hosed down with powerful streams of water and contents moved outside.
            c.   Perpetrator can use a timing device and establish an alibi.
            d.   Falling debris and building collapse may cover or destroy evidence.
            e.   Freezing weather makes searching for evidence difficult if everything becomes caked with ice.

    B.   Definitions.
        1.   Some states have included under arson laws the use of explosives to injure property.
        2.   *Corpus delicti* of arson (three elements).
            a.   Must be a fire or burning (depends on state whether mere scorching will meet this element).
            b.   Fire or burning was intentional.
            c.   Someone set the fire or caused it to be set.

II.   People as Sources of Information

    A.   Who discovered the fire?—Can report which part of the building was ablaze when s/he first noticed it.

    B.   Firefighters—Based on experience, they may be able to pinpoint the origin of structural fires.

C. Owner or manager of the structure—May need to be questioned twice: once to gather information about the building, possessions, etc., and again after other witnesses and evidence have been questioned and analyzed.

D. Employees—Generally know about business practices, safety issues, etc.

E. Insurance and financial personnel—Insurance fraud is a frequent motivation for arson.

F. Business competitors—Generally know the financial health of the industry.

G. Other possible witnesses.
    1. Spectators at the scene. Sometimes the perpetrator watches the fire.
    2. Neighbors and tenants.
    3. News media camera technicians; photographs of bystanders.
    4. Fortuitous witnesses. Interview those who routinely pass by the location.

III. Conducting the Investigation—Physical Evidence

A. Combustion—three components: fuel + oxygen + heat source = combustion.
    1. Fuels—Most are organic (carbon-based) and may produce carbon monoxide and carbon dioxide.
    2. Oxygen—If no ventilation to replace oxygen and reduce carbon dioxide and carbon monoxide, fire may extinguish itself.
    3. Heat sources.
        a. Accidental heat sources (heating/cooking, electrical, smoking).
        b. Natural heat sources (spontaneous combustion).
        c. Investigative significance (may be made to look accidental).
        d. Accelerants (gasoline, kerosene, lighter fluid, etc.).

B. Point of origin.
    1. Burn patterns.
        a. Pour patterns (pouring an accelerant onto floor).
        b. Alligatoring (pattern of blisters on wood).
        c. "V" pattern (pattern of burning or fanning out).
        d. Charring (the deeper the charring, the longer the burning).
    2. Heat distortion.
        a. Light bulbs (partially melted glass points in direction of fire).
        b. Spalling (cement crumbling, chalk-like appearance).
        c. Crazing (irregular pattern of lines in wood and glass).

  C.   Significance of finding point of origin.
        1.   Leads to possible ignition sources.
        2.   Finding of plants (i.e., timing devices, matches, trailers, or
              streamers).

  D.   Accelerants (gasoline is most common).
        1.   May be detected by visual observation, detecting scent, dye color
              tests, instrumental tests.
              a.   Gas chromatography.
              b.   Infrared spectrophotometry.
              c   Catalytic combustion/resistance analysis (sniffer).
        2.   Collection and transmission of accelerants to laboratory—safety
              precautions.

IV.   Motive

  A.   Financial gain.
        1.   Insurance fraud.
        2.   Elimination of competition.
        3.   Moving and resettlement allowance.

  B.   Intimidation.
        1.   Fear for safety (threats).
        2.   Threatened economic loss (labor disputes).
        3.   Change of policy (government attacks).

  C.   Emotional reasons.
        1.   Jealousy.
        2.   Spite.
        3.   Revenge.
        4.   Hatred.

  D.   Concealment of another crime.
        1.   Homicide.
        2.   Larceny.
        3.   Fraud, forgery, embezzlement.
        4.   Other crimes (i.e., burglaries and robberies).

  E.   Pyromania—irresistible impulse to start fires.

  F.   Recognition as a hero.

  G.   Vandalism (churches, schools, empty buildings).

V.   Records

    A.   Fire records.
          1. Location.
          2. Time and day of week.
          3. Name of occupants.
          4. Name of owners.
          5. Area of fire origin.
          6. Source of heat-causing ignition.
          7. Type of material ignited.
          8. Damage.

        9. Dollar amount of damage.

    B.   Straw owners—hidden ownership or financial interests in burned property.

Name: _____

Quiz

1. An estimated _____ percent of all structural fires in the United States are considered to be arson or of suspicious origin.

2. The reason photographs and videotapes should be taken of bystanders is that often one will find the same _____ at different fires.

3. The three components required of a fire are: a fuel, oxygen, and _____.

4. A device that ignites the first fuel or assists the initial flame to build in intensity is known as a(n) _____.

5. The most common cause of accidental fires is a(n) _____.

6. Burn patterns, heat distortion, and the observations of the first person who first noticed the fire are three sources of information that may help determine _____.

7. The most common accelerant used in arson is _____.

8. Intensity and duration of a fire may be determined by examining _____.

9. _____ is the irresistible impulse or compulsion to start a fire or set something on fire.

10. _____ is the term used for surface discoloration, chipping, crumbling, or a flaky, chalk-like appearance on cement.

Name: _____

CROSSWORD PUZZLE

CLUES

Across

1. The reaction of a chemical compound with oxygen.
4. Visible evidence of the exposure of cement to intense heat.
5. Another term for *trailers*.
7. A slang term for the catalytic combustion device.
8. Instrumental detection devices are based on established scientific principles such as _____ spectrophotometry.
12. Flame from a match or a cigarette lighter is the most common source for a(n) _____ fire.
14. A(n) _____ is a volatile liquid used to start fires and help them spread more rapidly.
15. _____ involves the intentional setting of a fire that results in the burning of a structure or property.
16. A distinctive burn blister pattern that resembles a reptile's hide.
17. A pattern or network of fine, irregular lines in glass or wood.

Down

1. Fuel + _____ + Heat Source = Combustion.

2. The temperature of the heat source must be greater than the _____ (or kindling) temperature of the fuel.

3. One of the underlying scientific principles that enable the operation of instrumental detection devices.

6. A _____ is used to extend the fire from the plant (or set) to other parts of the structure.

9. An irresistible impulse to start a fire or set something on fire.

10. A device that ignites the first fuel or assists the initial flame to build in intensity.

11. Together with oxygen and a heat source, _____ is the third essential component of a fire.

13. Many investigators believe that the deeper the _____, the longer the fire burned at that spot.

Chapter 20
Increasing Threats and Emerging Crime

LEARNING OBJECTIVES

1. Understand the new types of crimes that have evolved with technology and social changes.
2. Understand the new laws that have been enacted to deal with the new types of crimes.
3. Identify the legal requirements required to proceed with a criminal investigation.
4. Comprehend the purpose of INTERPOL and how it interacts with local law enforcement agencies.
5. Appreciate the efforts of the FBI's Public Awareness Campaign.
6. Understand the motives and illegal acts of religious movements and cult groups.

KEY TERMS AND CONCEPTS

identify theft
phishing
spoofing
INTERPOL
Satanism
cult
ritual crime
occult symbols
occult holidays or festivals

CHAPTER OUTLINE

I. Identity Theft

A. Phishing: computer scam in which a victim is contacted by e-mail or telephone and is asked for sensitive information that can be used to secure credit cards, open charge accounts, or otherwise defraud the victim.

B. Spoofing: efforts to obtain caller ID numbers for the victim's cell phone, which can then be used to obtain information about victim's identity.

II.   Internet Fraud

A.   Companies, employees, or former employees.

B.   In 2005, $336 billion was lost.

C.   61 percent of computers are infected with spyware.

III.   Exploitation of Women and Children

A.   Pornography.

B.   Human trafficking.

C.   Sexual exploitation.

D.   People smuggling.

E.   Child Pornography Protection Act (2001).

F.   INTERPOL.

IV.   Home Invasions

A.   Drugs.

B.   Elderly.

C.   Con games.

D.   Paintings/cultural objects.

V.   Body Parts

A.   Funeral parlors.

B.   Autopsies.

VI.   School Violence

A.   Government report on 10 key similarities between 1974 and 2000.

B.   Bullying and TV violence.

VII. Workplace Violence

    A.   Postal facilities.

    B.   The annual cost of workplace violence is $36 billion.

    C.   FBI's monograph for prevention, responding to events.

VIII. Satanism, Cults, and Ritual Crime

    A.   Definitions of terms used.

    B.   Media words and phrases used to describe crime-related events.

    C.   FBI — Kenneth Lanning's findings.

    D.   Self-styled Satanists.

    E.   Cults.

    F.   Religious movements.

    G.   Cult Awareness Network.

    H.   Mutilation.

    I.   Occult symbols and meanings.

    J.   Occult holidays.

Name: _____

QUIZ

1. A computer scam in which a victim is contacted by e-mail or telephone and is asked for his/her social security number , which can be used to defraud the victim, is called _____.

2. Efforts by criminals to obtain caller-ID numbers from the victim's cell phone, which can be used to obtain information about victim identity, is called: _____.

3. The organization that serves as a "clearinghouse" for information on the exploitation of women and children is _____

4. According to a 1994 study, the national annual cost of workplace violence is _____ .

5. In the United States most of the illegal trafficking in body parts centers on the illegal removal of organs sold by _____

6. According to the text, the definition of "Evil One" is _____.

7. According to the text, the scene of a ritual ceremony will usually be bounded by a circle _____ feet in diameter.

8. The name of the hand sign employed as a sign of recognition by those involved in occult matters is called the _____.

9. According to a report, 61 percent of computers in the United States are infected with _____.

10. According to the text, one of the occult holidays is Halloween, which is also known as _____.

Name: _____

CROSSWORD PUZZLE

CLUES

Across

1. Efforts by criminals to obtain caller identification numbers for the victim's cell phones, which can be used to obtain information about the victim's identity.
4. Experimental Satanist.
6. A rite initially fashioned by "fallen away" priests to express religious hatred.
10. The supreme spirit of evil; Satan, the prince of evil, is called the _____.
11. A goat's head located inside an inverted pentagram within the smaller of two concentric circles.
12. One of the fastest growing crimes in the United States.
13. _____ violence drew national attention in the 1990s, following a series of shootings in postal facilities.
14. The body of principles, articles of faith, or accepted belief that governs a social movement, institution, large group, or individual.

Down

1. A characteristic of _____ Satanists includes a preoccupation with death, a tendency to be a loner, an underachiever, and a user of narcotics.
2. Fake prescription medicines have been offered on the market by the _____.
3. An organized group dedicated to the same ideal, person, or thing.
5. Any practice that asserts secret or supernatural powers, disclosed only to the initiated.
7. An organized group dedicated to the same ideal, person, or thing.
8. A computer scam in which a victim is contacted by e-mail and is asked for social security number or other sensitive information.
9. The Book of _____ is the private, journal record of the ritualistic or occult activities of an individual or group.

Chapter 21
Terrorism

CHAPTER OUTLINE

I.   Introduction and Overview

    A.   Types of terrorism.
- 1. International terrorism—direction by a foreign government.
- 2. Domestic terrorism—group of two or more people whose activities are directed at elements of the U.S. government or population (no foreign direction).
- 3. Violent political movements.
- 4. Single-issue/special interest movements.
- 5. Racial and religious movements.
- 6. Global-economic movements.
- 7. Hate group movements.

    B.   Two aspects of terrorism of interest to investigators.
- 1. Recognition that terrorist activities have the capability to kill or injure large numbers of people.
- 2. The most effective investigations of terrorism are aimed at prevention (proactive).

    C.   Definition: The use of force or the fear of force to achieve a political or criminal end.

    D.   Result of 9/11 attacks on the United States.
- 1. Criticism of shared information between agencies.
- 2. Establishment of the Department of Homeland Security.
- 3. USA PATRIOT Act.

    E.   Historical terrorism in the United States.
- 1. Modern-day terrorism in the United States has its roots in the 1960s and 1970s during the Vietnam War.
- 2. Historical terrorism in the United States includes Ku Klux Klan, organized labor, anti-strike groups.
- 3. Most terrorist attacks in the United States are carried out by a small group—even one or two individuals.
- 4. Terrorism itself is not a crime, but rather a phenomenon accompanying more traditional crime (i.e., murder, bombing, kidnapping). Definitions of terrorism are vague and do not provide a clear *corpus delicti* for the crime.

    F.   Narco-terrorism.
- 1. Related to illegal drug cartels.
- 2. Domestic gang and organized crime activities.

II. Legal Aspects

A. Conventions that exist that address certain issues related to terrorism.
   1. Specialized conventions—focus on certain types of offenses (i.e., diplomatic protection, taking of hostages, air piracy).
   2. Regularly scheduled conventions—may have issues relating to terrorism (i.e., extradition).

B. U.S. federal legislation.
   1. The Comprehensive Crime Control Act 1984 (hostage taking).
   2. Omnibus Diplomatic Security and Antiterrorism Act 1986.
   3. The USA PATRIOT Act (2001).

C. Constraints on intelligence-gathering activities.
   1. Concern for First Amendment rights violations that might occur with domestic intelligence operations.
   2. Standard of "reasonable suspicion" applied to determine if investigation is warranted.
   3. USA PATRIOT Act established broader approach and powers to intercept electronic information.

III. Terrorism Investigations

A. Terrorism vs. traditional investigations.
   1. Success depends largely on intelligence and analysis.
   2. Establishing a *prima facie* case using surveillance, informants, records.

B. Crime scene investigations.
   1. Problem with secondary explosive devices and booby traps.
   2. Terrorist usually wants to communicate what group was responsible for the attack.

C. Terrorist suspects—MO may vary from act to act.
   1. Know as much about group or person as possible (i.e., goals, structure, tactical approach, means of communication, propensity for violence).
   2. Background investigations.
   3. Maintain good communications with other agencies that may have information (i.e., Postal Inspectors, BATF, DEA, Customs, INS, Homeland Security, etc.).
   4. International terrorist groups—INTERPOL.

IV. Bombings

A. Reactive investigations—traditional after-the-fact investigations of explosions focus on the site of the detonation.
   1. Parts of the bomb may be traced to the source.
   2. Linking a series of bombings.
   3. Bomb parts can be compared to parts in the bomb factory once located.

B. Proactive investigations—gathering of evidence that proves (or disproves) the involvement of a suspected perpetrator.
   1. Surveillance.
   2. Use of informants.

C. Explosives.
   1. Ease of availability and manufacture.
   2. Types of devices.
      a. Car bombs.
      b. Fragmentation bombs.
      c. Letter bombs.
      d. Aircraft bombs.

D. Other devices and techniques.
   1. Shoulder-mounted missile-firing weapons (i.e., Stingers).
   2. Weapons of mass destruction.
      a. Nuclear.
      b. Biological.
      c. Chemical.

V. Terrorism Activities

A. Chemical terrorism.
   1. Sarin and Tabun (nerve gases).
   2. Mustard gas.
   3. Butyric acid gas (has been used against abortion clinics).
B. Ecological terrorism—ecotage (sabotage efforts by groups to protect the environment).
C. Assassination—usually by explosives or firearms.
D. Kidnapping.

VI. Strategic Initiatives

A. Records—individuals involved in terrorist activities are likely to have arrest records.
   1. Police records.
   2. Stolen-item records (for objects that may be related to terrorist activity).

    3. Military records.
    4. Vehicle sales and rentals.
    5. Weapons and explosives dealers.
    6. School records.
    7. Bank records.
    8. Airline records.

B. Other agencies.
    1. U.S. Secret Service (political threat letters).
    2. INS.
    3. BATF.
    4. U.S. Marshal's Service.
    5. U.S. Postal Inspection Service.
    6. FBI.

Name: _____

QUIZ

1. Most terrorist acts in the United States are investigated by what agency?

    _____

2. _____ is closely associated with drug cartels in Central and South America.

3. U.S. Congress passed _____ in 2002, which places greater controls on protection of food and water and enhances controls on biological agents and toxic substances.

4. According to the USA PATRIOT Act of 2001, it is a(n) _____ crime to use violence against any passenger on board an aircraft.

5. _____ entails the gathering of evidence that proves or disproves the involvement of a suspected perpetrator in a crime.

6. _____ is the term used to describe an after-the-fact investigation of a terrorist bomb explosion that focuses on the site of the detonation.

7. _____ is the term used for a location that is free of surveillance and can be used for illegal activities such as making bombs.

8. In the United States, the most common explosive device used by terrorist groups has been a(n) _____ made with black powder.

9. _____ terrorism involves efforts by groups to protect the environment.

10. Terrorism can defined as the use of force or the fear of force to achieve a(n) _____ end.

Name: _____

CROSSWORD PUZZLE

CLUES

Across

2. A terrorism _____ typically includes federal agents and state and local law enforcement officers working together with other elements of the criminal justice system.

3. _____ investigations are conducted after the terrorist event.

6. An investigator seeking a warrant typically must be able to show _____ suspicion that the subject(s) of the warrant is/are involved in criminal activity.

8. Another term for ecological terrorism.

10. An exception to the general rule that monetary gain is not a motivation for terrorism.

11. _____ bombs are usually designed to explode while in flight, ideally over water.
12. _____ terrorism generally involves direction by a foreign government.
14. The unlawful use or threat of violence against persons or property to further political or social objectives.
15. The international police organization.

Down

1. A _____, typically located near the ultimate target of a terrorist attack, is often used as a bomb factory.
4. _____ bombs are designed to kill or maim people.
5. _____ bombs are used to kill the occupants of a vehicle, those passing by a vehicle, or as so-called "suicide" bombs.
7. The _____ from any explosive device is capable of killing; the greater the amount of explosive used, the greater the damage.
9. _____ investigations focus on the gathering of evidence that proves (or disproves) the involvement of a suspected perpetrator in a crime.
13. _____ bombs consist of a relatively small amount of explosive, but enough to kill or maim.

Chapter 22
Computers and Technological Crime

KEY TERMS AND CONCEPTS

artificial intelligence
Automated Fingerprint Identification System (AFIS)
Central Processing Unit (CPU)
chat rooms
CLEAR
component service technician
cracker
cybercrime
cyberdetective
GPS
hacker
imaging
ISP
laptop
mainframe computer
mini-computer
personal computer (PC)
Rapid Start Team
read-only memory (ROM)
virus

Chapter Outline

I. Cybercrime

A. Crimes committed using computers and/or the Internet.
1. Child pornography and exploitation.
2. Economic-related fraud.
3. Prostitution.
4. Gambling.
5. Extortion.
6. Electronic stalking and harassment.
7. Illegal drug activities.
8. Telecommunications fraud.
9. Identity theft.
10. Software theft.

B. Electronic apparatus.
1. Cell phones.
2. PDAs.
3. DVD recorders.
4. Digital cameras.
5. Scanners.
6. Personal computers.

II. Legal Issues

A. Internet.
1. Laws vary from state to state.
2. Search warrants generally required.

B. Primary issues to right to privacy.
1. Home computers.
2. Workplace computers.
3. Internet service providers (ISPs).
4. Chat rooms.
5. Web sites.

III. Investigating High-Tech and IT Crime

A. Protection of scene.
1. Calling of a competent service technician.
2. Protection against viruses.
3. Protection against self-destruct systems.

B. Destruction of evidence.
1. Do not turn computer off or on.
2. Do not ask suspect to assist with computer.

C. Child pornography and exploitation.
    1. Correlation between child molesters and people selling or trading in child pornography.
    2. Stalking and harassment.

D. Economic crimes.
    1. Business fraud and embezzlement.
    2. Stolen/forged credit cards.
    3. Identity theft.
    4. Fraudulent wire transfers, bank fraud, telecommunications fraud, money laundering.
    5. Economic espionage and stealing trade secrets.

E. Computer hacking and cracking.
    1. Hacking: entering computer system illegally or without the knowledge of the victim.
    2. Cracking: entering computer system illegally or without the knowledge of the victim with intent to commit a crime.
    3. Viruses.

F. Computer sabotage.
    1. Destroying business database is goal.
    2. Types of programs used.
        a. Clipper chip—computer chip designed for encryption.
        b. Encryption—protects communication and electronic commerce.
        c. Logic bomb—virus that is dormant until a particular time.
        d. Pinging—form of vandalism or sabotage using e-mail remailing.
        e. Remailer—sends thousands of messages to an e-mail address.
        f. Trapdoor—bypasses security controls of a computer's mainframe system.
        g. Trojan horse—software embedded in a popular and trusted computer software program that steals secrets or modifies the database. Not considered a virus because it does not replicate itself and spread.
        h. Virus—software that infects a computer system and spreads from one computer to another.
        i. Worm—software that works its way through to a single computer system or network, changing and destroying data or codes.

G. Other criminal uses.
    1. Illegal drug activity.

2. Telecommunications fraud—stolen cell phone numbers.
3. Terrorism—Internet is primary means of communication.

IV. Computer Crime Investigation and the Electronic Crime Scene

A. Observe and document the physical scene.
   1. Position of components (i.e., mouse).
   2. Condition of computer system (i.e., off or on).

B. Photograph scene.
   1. 360-degree coverage of room.
   2. Front of computer and monitor.

C. Handling of computer components.
   1. Do not turn computer on or off.
   2. Do not ask suspect to assist with computer.

V. Law Enforcement Uses of IT

A. Databases.
   1. Fingerprints and AFIS.
   2. MO files.
   3. Stolen property files.
   4. FBI Rapid Start Team.
   5. Crime pattern analysis.

B. Electronic surveillance.
   1. Wiretaps.
   2. Voice paging.
   3. Cell phone intercepts.
   4. Pen registers.
   5. Internet or computer communications intercepts.

C. Resources on the Web.
   1. FBI.
   2. U.S. Treasury.
   3. INTERPOL.
   4. U.S. Postal Inspection Service.
   5. American Society for Industrial Security (ASIS).
   6. Internet Fraud Complaint Center (IFCC).
   7. Department of Homeland Security.
   8. National Counterintelligence Center (NACIC).

Name: _____

Quiz

1. Police investigators may pose as children in _____ in an effort to draw out sex offenders.

2. According to the text, _____ costs $55 billion a year globally, making it a bigger business than international drug trafficking.

3. _____ are individuals who illegally enter computer systems to destroy, change, or steal data.

4. _____ is a security loophole analysis program designed for use by system administrators to detect insecure systems.

5. _____ are e-mails containing live data intended to cause damage to the recipient computer.

6. A type of computer sabotage software that works its way through a single computer system or a network, changing and destroying data or codes, is called a(n) _____.

7. Law enforcement personnel posing as minors in "chat rooms" to draw out pedophiles has not been considered as _____ by the courts.

8. One of the fastest-growing areas of computer crime is _____.

9. The fingerprint search and identification system noted in the text is known as _____.

10. The investigator facing a crime scene involving computers should protect the area and call for a(n) _____.

Name: _____

CROSSWORD PUZZLE

CLUES

Across

2. Handheld personal digital assistant (abbrev.).
7. A common defense attempted by pedophiles captured by police posing as children in chat rooms.
9. _____ are specialists who bring a new dimension to the field of crime investigation.
10. Automated Fingerprint Identification System (abbrev.).
11. _____ theft is one of the fastest-growing crimes in the United States.
12. One who enters a computer illegally for the purpose of destroying, changing, or stealing data.

Down

1. One who enters a computer illegally without the knowledge of the victim.
3. Software that works its way through a single computer system, changing and destroying data.

4. A concept called _____ intelligence is used for sophisticated data manipulation.

5. Can provide information on location, velocity, bearing, direction, and track of movement.

6. Software that "infects" a computer and spreads from one computer to another.

8. A(n) _____ computer is typically referred to as a PC.

Chapter 23
Enterprise Crime:
Organized, Economic, and White-Collar Crime

LEARNING OBJECTIVES

1. Understand the modern definition of enterprise crime.
2. Explain how an enterprise criminal differs from a traditional criminal.
3. Describe the proper procedures for investigating criminal activity associated with enterprise crime.
4. Identify and discuss which organized criminal groups operate in the United States.
5. Identify some of the developing areas in which enterprise criminals might emerge.
6. Understand the significant changes and trends that have developed in drug and drug-trafficking investigations.
7. Comprehend the investigative value of the RICO and asset forfeiture laws.

KEY TERMS AND CONCEPTS

angel dust
asset forfeiture
cocaine
la Cosa Nostra
crack cocaine
crack houses
Crips and Bloods
cutouts
drug cartels
enterprise crime
heroin
Jamaican Posses
Mafia
marijuana
money laundering
Racketeer-Influenced Corrupt Organizations (RICO) law
PCP
Rastafarian
reverse directory
safe houses
surveillance
triad
triangular model
turnarounds

CHAPTER OUTLINE

I.   Introduction

The primary goals of individuals involved in enterprise crime are:

A.   Propagation of the group.

B.   Financial or economic gain.

C.   The advancement of power and influence.

II.   People—The Enterprise Criminal

A.   Differences between enterprise criminals and traditional criminals.
1.   They represent a greater threat to society.
2.   They are much more difficult to investigate.
3.   They are usually self-perpetuating.

B.   Criminal groups.
1.   Are usually hierarchical in nature.
2.   Exclusive membership.
3.   Operate within own code of behavior.

C.   Types of groups.
1.   Mafia (*la Cosa Nostra*).
2.   Asian gangs (offshoots of the Triads in Asia).
3.   Yakuza (Japan).
4.   United Bamboo Gang (Taiwan).
5.   Colombian drug cartels.
6.   Warlords (Myanmar).

III.   Conducting the Investigation

A.   Laws—in some cases it may be necessary to pass new laws and develop new procedures to control enterprise crime.
1.   Asset forfeiture—one of the most effective laws.
2.   Other procedures.

B.   Primary areas of interest.
1.   Organization and structure of the group—most groups are hierarchical.
2.   Membership of the group—traditional group membership is strictly controlled. Many newer groups are built around family relationships. Some criminal gangs recruit from prison.

3. Sphere of influence of individuals the group works with or controls—most active enterprise crime groups could not survive without corrupt governmental officials. Blackmail is often used to keep corrupt officials in line.
4. Goals or purpose of the group—knowing how the group works provides a basis for a criminal case. May use "smoke screens" to cover up or use go-betweens to actually carry out criminal activities.
5. The means by which the group attains its goals.

IV. Typology of Enterprise Criminality

A. The Mafia.
   1. Also known as *la Cosa Nostra* ("our thing"), the syndicate, the mob.
   2. Roots in Sicily.
   3. Violent organization that preys largely on the failures of human nature.

B. Colombian drug-trafficking organizations.
   1. Most notorious are the Medellin and Cali drug cartels.
   2. Cartels are groups of independent organizations that work together on various levels (supply, distribution, trafficking, etc.).
   3. Considered one of the fastest-growing groups in the United States.
   4. Money laundering is one of the major concerns.

C. Jamaican Posses.
   1. Involved mainly with drug dealing and firearms trafficking.
   2. Active in burglaries, robberies, fraud, and auto theft.
   3. Originated in Kingston, Jamaica.
   4. Some degree of rivalry between groups and little loyalty.
   5. Sometimes confused with the Rastafarians of Jamaica, who smoke marijuana as part of their religion.

D. Asian criminal groups.
   1. Chinese criminal organizations—Tongs. Many are listed as social organizations and are involved in legitimate as well as illegal activities. As many as 30 Tongs are operating in the United States, each with its own membership rules and independent structures.
   2. Viet Ching and Vietnamese groups—thought to be made up of former members of Vietnamese armed forces and criminals from Vietnam. Adult gangs are violent and involved in murder, extortion, arson, and fraud. Youth gangs operate much like traditional street gangs. They are involved in burglary, robbery, and other street crimes. Both groups are mainly active in their own communities.
   3. Triads—refers to the relationship between heaven, earth, and humankind. Little activity in the United States. Each member is given a number divisible by three.

E. Street gangs.
1. Bloods and Crips—viewed as most violent in U.S. history.
2. Involved in extensive forms of criminal activity.
3. Number of individuals involved in street gangs in the U.S. may exceed 200,000.
4. Many gangs are racially or ethnically structured.

V. New Developments in Crime

A. Illegal drugs and drug trafficking.

B. Computer-related crime.

C. Theft of technology, industrial espionage.

D. Arms dealing.

E. Art and cultural object theft.

F. Dealing in body parts, such as kidneys and hearts.

G. Kidnapping, slavery, and prostitution in new forms.

H. Mail fraud.

VI. Investigation of Illegal Drugs and Drug Trafficking

A. Traditional investigations.
1. Two aspects that are different from investigations of other forms of crime.
   a. The need to secure evidence to establish *corpus delicti*.
   b. The frequent need to protect witnesses from drug dealers.
2. Witnesses may also be drug dealers, providing information as a means to eliminate competition.

B. Surveillance.
1. Represents the most effective means of collecting information.
2. Problem with surveillance—the use of code words in conversations by some groups.

C. Undercover and informant operations.
1. An effective means of collecting information.
2. Involves a high degree of specialization and training.
3. High degree of care must be undertaken.

D. Cooperative investigations.
1. Establishment of task forces has become commonplace.
2. Multijurisdictional agencies working together.
3. Problem with conflicts in policies and procedures with different agencies.

E. International investigations.
1. Overseas agents of DEA, Customs, Postal Service, FBI.
2. U.S. agents work with counterparts in other nations.
3. CIA and military assist in investigations.
4. INTERPOL and EUROPOL serve as data-collection agencies and information exchange points.

F. Drugs.
1. Common drugs encountered.
    a. Cocaine.
    b. Crack cocaine.
    c. Heroin.
    d. Marijuana.
    e. PCP (angel dust).
    f. Others (amphetamines, barbiturates, "designer" drugs).
2. Codes.
    a. Cutouts—individuals who know nothing other than the message being passed.
    b. Use of reverse directories for frequently called phone numbers.

VII. RICO and Asset Forfeiture in the Investigative Process

A. RICO—Racketeer Influenced Corrupt Organizations laws apply to a wide range of organized criminal activity.
1. Seize property used in violation of the law or bought with illegal money.
2. Seizure does not require a conviction of the crime.
3. Asset forfeiture.

B. CCE—Continuing Criminal Enterprise statute. Makes it a crime if six or more persons, acting in concert, commit a continuing series of felonies under the 1970 Drug Abuse Prevention and Control Act. Series involves at least three related violations.

Name: _____

QUIZ

1.   Enterprise crime is characterized by illegal relationships and

     _____.

2.   Enterprise criminal groups are usually hierarchical in nature, have an
     exclusive membership, and operate within their own _____

     _____.

3.   _____ makes it possible to seize a crimi-
     nal's property or valuables that were used in criminal enterprise.

4.   It is estimated that the number of individuals involved in street gangs in the
     United States may exceed _____.

5.   _____ is a term that refers to the relationship between
     heaven, earth, and humankind.

6.   The _____ is/are a Jamaican group that
     smokes marijuana as part of their religion.

7.   The Mafia, with origins in Sicily, is also known as "our thing" or

     _____.

8.   According to the text, _____ is the most effective
     means of collecting information in drug-related investigations.

9.   Multijurisdictional law enforcement agencies that combine to investigate
     enterprise criminal activities are sometimes referred to as

     _____.

10. Drug cartels are characterized by extreme violence, corruption of officials,
     and even _____.

Name: _____

CROSSWORD PUZZLE

CLUES

Across

1. Asset _____ forms the basis of one of the most effective recent laws against enterprise crime.
6. Racketeer Influenced Corrupt Organizations.
8. *La Cosa Nostra*.
10. A natural product derived from the leaves of the coca plant.
13. A term for informants.
15. A(n) _____ directory provides the location where a telephone is connected.
16. Another term for rock cocaine is _____ cocaine.

Down

2. A member of a Jamaican group whose members smoke marijuana as part of their religious practice.
3. _____ crime includes a much broader range of criminal activity than what is commonly thought of as traditional organized crime.
4. _____ makes up most of the work of drug investigators.
5. Made from the dried leaves of the hemp plant.

7. _____ Posses are involved primarily in drug dealing and firearms trafficking.

9. Money _____ is a major concern to the drug cartels.

10. Individuals who know nothing more than the message being passed.

11. The Medellin and Cali _____ control approximately 80 percent of the cocaine distributed in the United States.

12. _____ dust is a street name for PCP.

13. _____ societies date back more than 100 years in China.

14. Phencyclidine.

Chapter 24

The Automobile and Crime

LEARNING OBJECTIVES

1. Understand the difference between larceny and fraud.
2. Discuss the most common reasons why automobiles are stolen.
3. Discuss the methods car thieves use to obtain and re-sell stolen cars and car parts.
4. Discuss unique investigative concerns and processes related to motor vehicle theft.
5. Describe indicators that might alert a patrol officer to the fact that a vehicle observed in traffic may be stolen.
6. Define carjacking and explain the difference between carjacking and motor vehicle larceny.
7. Discuss unique investigative concerns and processes related to carjacking.

KEY TERMS AND CONCEPTS

carjacking
chop shop
drive-by shooting
fraud
joyriding
larceny
phantom car claim
title switching
Vehicle Identification Number (VIN)

CHAPTER OUTLINE

I. **Auto Theft**

    A. Larceny—composed of three elements:
        1. The taking and removing,
        2. Of another's personal property,
        3. With intent, permanently, to deprive the owner of its use.

    B. Fraud—involves deception to achieve an unlawful gain.

II. **Why Motor Vehicles Are Stolen**

    A. Joyriding—youthful offenders.

    B.   Transportation.
        1.   Committing another felony—getaway car, drive-by shootings.
        2.   Transitory needs—runaways, hitchhikers.

    C.   Profit motive.
        1.   Organized theft rings.
            a.   Steal-to-order groups.
            b.   Chop shops—parts dismantled and sold to legitimate body shops.
        2.   Resale.
            a.   Fraudulent title or legal restriction.
            b.   Title switching—stealing car that matches a wrecked one and substituting titles and VIN plates.
        3.   Insurance fraud.
            a.   False claims.
            b.   Phantom car claims—forged title to a nonexistent car used to obtain insurance and then report as stolen.
            c.   Insuring wrecks—variation of the phantom car claim fraud.

III. Investigating Motor Vehicle Theft

    A.   Reasons cases are difficult to solve.
        1.   Crime is easy to commit.
        2.   Hard to trace stripped parts.
        3.   Many offenders are joyriders or use the vehicle temporarily.
        4.   Car theft rings are usually organized and sophisticated.
        5.   Diminished resources due to crime against property.

    B.   Computer correlation analysis—if stolen vehicle matches one used in another crime.

    C.   Recovered cars.
        1.   Motive greatly influences whether a stolen car will be recovered.
        2.   Identifying the vehicle—Vehicle Identification Number (VIN).
        3.   Searching the vehicle—fingerprints, discarded items, DNA from saliva and other body fluids.

    D.   Follow-up.
        1.   Patrol force.
            a.   Driver behavior or appearance.
            b.   Condition of vehicle.
        2.   Record checks.
        3.   Detectives.
            a.   Abandoned vehicles.
            b.   Vehicle intact or with major damage?
            c.   Joyriders.
            d.   Transportation needs.
            e.   Vehicle stripped.

IV. People, Physical Evidence, and Records

- A. People.
    1. Interviewing complainant.
    2. Interviewing neighbors, juveniles, gang members.
    3. Interviewing body shop and salvage yard owners.
    4. NATB.
    5. Insurance investigators.
    6. Suspects and suspects' friends and families.

- B. Physical evidence.
    1. Task for the criminalist.
    2. Toolmarks.
    3. Serial number restoration.

- C. Records.
    1. State department of motor vehicles.
    2. Insurance company records.
    3. INTERPOL on shipping of motor vehicles to other countries.

V. Carjacking

- A. Definition—the attempted or completed robbery of the victim's motor vehicle by a stranger to the victim.

- B. Victim characteristics.
    1. Follows same characteristics as in other violent crime patterns.
    2. Blacks victimized more often than whites.
    3. Men victimized more often than women.
    4. Single victimized more often than married.
    5. Victims usually under age 50.

- C. Incident/offender characteristics.
    1. Males most likely to commit.
    2. Nonwhites most likely to commit.
    3. Completed attempts during daylight hours.

- D. Carjacking murders and abductions.
    1. Offender usually unaware that infants are present in car until after the act.
    2. Murders are rare.

- E. Investigating carjacking.
    1. People—victim is an eyewitness.
    2. Records.
    3. Physical evidence.

Name: _____

QUIZ

1. The act of driving up to a gas station, asking for a "fill-up," and then leaving without paying would constitute _____.

2. _____ are places where stolen cars are dismantled and their parts sold to legitimate body shops.

3. The serial number of a motor vehicle is known as the _____.

4. A significant number of vehicles are stolen by juveniles looking for a dare or for racing thrills. This is called _____.

5. _____ is the attempted or completed robbery of the victim's motor vehicle by a stranger to the victim.

6. Most successful carjackings occur during _____ hours.

7. Two kinds of stealing cars for profit are those who steal cars for resale and those who steal cars for _____.

8. A type of insurance fraud in which the offender uses a forged title to an nonexistent vehicle to obtain insurance and then make a claim of auto theft is known as a(n) _____.

9. One reason auto theft is difficult to investigate is that many offenders (i.e., joyriders and those looking for temporary transportation) are quick to _____ the vehicle.

10. _____ may be contacted with regard to information on shipment of vehicles to other countries.

Chapter 25
Managing Criminal Investigations

LEARNING OBJECTIVES

1. Appreciate the historical antecedents to criminal law enforcement and investigation.
2. Understand and describe conventional investigative arrangements.
3. Understand and explain the concept of Managing Criminal Investigations (MCI).
4. Identify the five significant elements in the management of criminal investigations.
5. Appreciate the potential benefits of the MCI concept.
6. Understand how psychology plays an important role in the making of a good investigator.

KEY TERMS AND CONCEPTS

case monitoring system
case screening
CompStat
generalists
initial investigation
Managing Criminal Investigations (MCI)
SATCOM
solvability factors
specialists

CHAPTER OUTLINE

I. **Historical Antecedents**

    A. Law enforcement delegated to the states rather than being nationalized in the United States.

    B. Crime was local in nature.

    C. Each state enacted penal laws and turned over the enforcement and prosecution of them to counties and subdivisions.

II.   Conventional Investigative Arrangements

A.   Policy of political consideration and friendship on detective selection.
1.   Promotes corruption within detective bureau.
2.   Promotes alienation of detectives from the rest of police department.

B.   Traditional organization of detective bureaus.
1.   Specialists (i.e., homicide, auto theft, burglary).
2.   Generalists.

III.   Managing Criminal Investigations (MCI)

A.   Four considerations that govern any assessment of the investigative function.
1.   Number of arrests.
2.   Number of cases cleared.
3.   Number of convictions.
4.   Number of cases accepted for prosecution.

B.   Elements of MCI.
1.   The initial investigation.
2.   Case screening.
3.   Management of the ongoing investigation.
4.   Police-prosecutor relations.
5.   Continuous monitoring of the investigative process.

C.   The initial investigation.
1.   Difference between traditional investigation efforts and MCI.
   a.   Traditional—initial investigation performed by detectives.
   b.   MCI—initial investigation performed by the patrol officer responding to the call.
2.   Need for patrol officers to be trained in collection and preservation of physical evidence.

D.   Case screening.
1.   Solvability factors.
   a.   Is there a witness?
   b.   Is a suspect named?
   c.   Can a suspect be described?
   d.   Can a suspect be located?
   e.   Can a suspect vehicle be identified?
   f.   Is stolen property traceable?
   g.   Is physical evidence present?
   h.   Is there a distinguishable MO?

2. Certain solvability factors weigh heavier than others (i.e., a named suspect would have a "heavier weight" than would a distinguishable MO).

3. If case is recommended "closed" due to low solvability factors, supervisors use "case screening" to remove the case from the workload.

E. Management of the continuing investigation.
1. Delegating more investigative responsibility to patrol force.
2. Eliminating uneven workloads among detectives.

F. Police-prosecutor relations.
1. Traditional practice for police to act independently within the criminal justice system.
2. MCI encourages mutual cooperation among agencies, five essential steps.
   a. Increase consultation between executives of the agencies.
   b. Increase cooperation among supervisory personnel of the agencies.
   c. Use of liaison officers.
   d. Improve case preparation procedures.
   e. Develop a system of formal and informal feedback to the police on case dispositions.

G. Investigative monitoring systems.
1. Provides continuous feedback on the investigative process and quality of personnel performance.
2. Monitoring problems (i.e., process might be sabotaged by personnel).

IV. Potential Benefits and Drawbacks of MCI

A. Increase in productivity through better use of available resources.

B. Reallocation of the resources made available through case screening.
1. Proactive investigations.
2. Formation of task force units.
3. Better case preparation for prosecution.

C. Rejection of favoritism as the basis of selection of detectives.

V. Introduction of CompStat

A. CompStat is a statistical mapping program first used by the New York City Police Department in the 1990s.

B. CompStat is designed to analyze and measure criminal activity and police performance within a given geographic area.

C.   It has expanded to other programs, such as SATCOM (Strategic and Tactical Command), which combines databases on career criminals.

VI. The Psychology of Crime Investigation

A.   Mind-set is a posture an investigator should take to:
1.   Avoid jumping to conclusions.
2.   Avoid formulating opinions based on prior experience.
3.   Control for personal biases.

B.   Problem of investigators failing to understand their own personal psychological makeup.

C.   Cognition is the process of acquiring knowledge by use of reason, intuition, or perception.

D.   Personality – id, superego, ego.

E.   Observation.

Name: _____

QUIZ

1. Detective bureaus have traditionally been organized into
    _____ and specialists.

2. MCI requires that the initial investigation be performed by
    _____.

3. _____ is the process that removes cases from
    the workload, thus making resources available for those cases holding
    greater promise.

4. Case monitoring systems are set up to give administrators continuous feed-
    back on investigative process and _____.

5. Detectives who handled specific types of crimes are called
    _____.

6. According to the text, if MCI is to work, patrol officers may need addi-
    tional training in _____.

7. Empirical research has identified _____;
    the presence of such suggests that a solution is possible if the case is pur-
    sued by detectives.

8. Using an investigative monitoring system allows supervisors to build a pro-
    file of each detective's abilities, assess their productivity, and
    _____.

9. MCI requires that there be a good _____
    between the police and other agencies in the criminal justice system.

10. One of the benefits of using MCI is eliminating the traditional use of
    _____ as a means of selecting detectives.

Chapter 26
Control Over Investigations Through Constitutional Law

Learning Objectives

1. Appreciate the historical development of constitutional law and its importance to criminal investigation.
2. Identify the limitations placed on the powers of the federal government by the Bill of Rights.
3. Develop an awareness of the significance of the Preamble to the Constitution, the Articles, and the Bill of Rights to the criminal investigation process.
4. Describe the role of the Supreme Court as it pertains to the field of criminal justice.
5. Comprehend the importance of the incorporation of the Bill of Rights through the Fourteenth Amendment.
6. Identify and understand the milestone decisions affecting the criminal investigative process.
7. Appreciate the evolution and significance of the underlying principles of probable cause.

Key Terms and Concepts

Bill of Rights
crime suppression model
Declaration of Independence
due process
due process model
equal protection
executive branch
ex post facto law
judicial branch
judicial restraint
legislative branch
Preamble to the Constitution
probable cause
seizable property
treason
Wickersham Commission
writ of *habeas corpus*
writ of *mandamus*

CHAPTER OUTLINE

I. Historical Perspectives

A. Limiting power of federal government.
1. Declaration of Independence.
2. Articles of Confederation.

B. U.S. Constitution.
1. Bill of Rights—first 10 amendments
2. Fourteenth Amendment provided a Constitutional basis for the federal government to intervene in a state criminal matter.

II. The Constitution and Criminal Justice

A. The Preamble.

B. The articles and amendments.
1. Article I—the legislative branch.
2. Article II—the executive branch.
3. Article III—the judicial branch.
4. Article IV—the states and its citizens.
5. Article V—the supreme law of the land.

C. The Bill of Rights.
1. Fourth Amendment—search and seizure.
2. Fifth Amendment—witness against self, double jeopardy, due process of law.
3. Sixth Amendment—speedy, impartial jury and assistance of counsel.
4. Eighth Amendment—excessive bail, fines, cruel and unusual punishment.
5. Ninth Amendment—any right not expressly mentioned in the first eight amendments.
6. Tenth Amendment—criminal justice reserved for the states.
7. Fourteenth Amendment—applies the Constitution to the states, equal protection of the laws.

III. The Supreme Court and Criminal Justice

A. Article III, Section 1 of the Constitution—one Supreme Court.
1. *Marbury v. Madison*—the Court has no power to issue a writ of *mandamus* under the Judiciary Act of 1789.
2. *Martin v. Hunter's Lessee* and *Cohens v. Virginia*—right of the Court to review lower courts' rulings.

B.   Incorporating the Bill of Rights through the Fourteenth Amendment.
1.   Pre-Civil-War issues.
2.   Post-Civil-War issues.
3.   New Deal era, changing interpretations of the Constitution.
4.   The Wickersham Commission.
5.   Judicial restraint—narrow interpretation of the Constitution.
6.   The Earl Warren Court (1953-1969).

IV.   **Milestone Decisions Affecting Investigative Practice**

A.   *Rochin v. California*—overzealous police practices.

B.   *Gideon v. Wainwright*—right to counsel.

V.   **Probable Cause: Its Evolution and Significance**

A.   Arrests without warrants.
1.   Crimes committed in officer's presence.
2.   Certain crimes upon probable cause.
3.   Seizable property—contraband, fruits of the crime, instruments of the crime.
4.   Fourth Amendment—term "probable cause" appears.

B.   Meaning of probable cause.
1.   *Locke v. United States*—suspicion.
2.   *Stacey v. Emery*—prudent, cautious.
3.   *Carroll v. United States* and *Brinegar v. United States*—reasonable.
4.   *Johnson v. United States*—arrest not justified by what the subsequent search discloses.
5.   Crime suppression model vs. due process model of criminal justice.

Name: _____

QUIZ

1. The _____ Amendment grants the Supreme Court a constitutional basis to intervene in a state criminal matter.

2. Excessive bail, excessive fines, and cruel and unusual punishment are restricted under the _____ Amendment.

3. The first 10 amendments to the U.S. Constitution are known as _____.

4. The right to a speedy and public trial by an impartial jury is found under the _____ Amendment.

5. Past Supreme Court decisions having the greatest influence on investigative practices are based on the _____, _____, _____, and _____ Amendments.

6. *Gideon v. Wainwright* focused on the right to _____.

7. The definition of probable cause was expanded from prudent, cautious suspicion to reasonable suspicion in *Carroll v. United States* and _____.

8. Property that constitutes contraband, fruits of a crime, instruments of a crime, or other relevant evidence is known as _____.

9. The case of _____ established that justification of an arrest cannot be based on what is disclosed in a subsequent search.

10. Law enforcement reasoning of the law is based on a crime suppression model, whereas the Court's reasoning is based on a(n) _____.

NAME: _____

CROSSWORD PUZZLE

CLUES

Across

2. The Fourteenth Amendment includes the clause guaranteeing all persons "_____ of the laws."

4. With the exception of _____, no crime is defined in the Constitution.

5. The Fourth Amendment requires the establishment of _____ cause as the basis for issuance of a search warrant.

7. When seeking a search warrant, the applicant must believe that _____ property will be found.

10. The 1931 National Commission on Law Observance and Enforcement was more commonly known as the _____ Commission.

11. The legalistic school advocates judicial _____, whereby the U.S. Supreme Court confines its supervisory power over law enforcement practice to federal agencies and procedure.

12. Article I of the U.S. Constitution prohibits suspension of the writ of _____.

Down

1. The Fourteenth Amendment bars any state from depriving "any person of life, liberty, or property, without _____ of law."
2. Article I of the U.S. Constitution prohibits passage of any _____ law.
3. Article II of the Constitution addresses matters relative to the _____ branch of the government.
6. Article III of the Constitution addresses matters relative to the _____ branch of the government.
7. Many in the law enforcement profession advocate a crime _____ model of criminal justice, which places them at odds with the U.S. Supreme Court's favor of a due process model.
8. Article I of the Constitution addresses matters relative to the _____ branch of the government.
9. In *Marbury v. Madison*, the U.S. Supreme Court ruled the Judiciary Act of 1789 unconstitutional in giving the Court the power to issue a writ of _____.

Chapter 27
Evidence and Effective Testimony

LEARNING OBJECTIVES

1. Understand and explain what is considered to be evidence.
2. Appreciate the historical background of the rules of evidence.
3. Identify and explain what is meant by rules of evidence.
4. Understand the importance of effective testimony.
5. Identify the primary purposes of cross-examination by the defense counsel.

KEY TERMS AND CONCEPTS

Anglican system
circumstantial evidence
competency
cross-examination
demonstrative evidence
direct evidence
effective testimony
inquisitorial system
leading questions
materiality
objection as to form
objection as to substance
real evidence
relevancy
testimonial evidence

CHAPTER OUTLINE

I. **Introduction—What is Evidence?**

    A. Investigator's responsibility.
        1. Establish that a crime was committed.
        2. Develop evidence to prove beyond a reasonable doubt that a particular individual is guilty of that crime.

    B. Type of evidence.
        1. Testimonial evidence—given orally by a witness.
        2. Real evidence—any tangible object or exhibit offered as proof.
        3. Demonstrative evidence—charts, drawings, models, etc.

      4. Direct evidence—evidence that, in itself, proves or refutes the fact at issue.

      5. Circumstantial evidence—indirect proof from which a fact at issue may be inferred (i.e., most forensic evidence).

II. Historical Background of the Rules of Evidence

A. Two dominant systems of justice.
1. Romanesque (1200 A.D.)—Known as the inquisitorial system. Judge dominated and directed. Few rules governed procedure.
2. Anglican (England)—Used in the United States. Adversarial system using a jury of peers and an elaborate set of procedural rules.

B. Developments in the Unites States.
1. Rules of evidence established by the legislature.
2. Rules of evidence established by court decisions.

III. The Rules of Evidence

A. Relevant evidence—first prong in test for admissibility.
1. Concerned with whether there is a connection between the evidence and the issue to be proved.
2. Tends to prove or disprove a fact.

B. Material evidence—second prong in test for admissibility.
1. Means to have probative weight.
2. All material evidence is relevant but all relevant evidence is not necessarily material.

C. Competent evidence—third prong in test for admissibility.
1. Constitutional grounds—evidence may be relevant and material but incompetent as determined by the courts.
2. Statutory incompetence—evidence not admissible under a state or federal statute, prohibiting its admissibility (i.e., wiretaps, privileged communication).

IV. What Is Effective Testimony?

A. Understandable testimony.
1. Use lay terms, avoid police jargon.
2. Clear, distinct voice.

B. Believable testimony.
1. First-hand knowledge, preparedness to answer questions.
2. Do not appear overzealous.
3. Show compassion for victim and accused.

C.   Behavior and appearance.
    1.   Demeanor and conduct in behavior.
    2.   Appearance, grooming.

V.   Cross-Examination

A.   Purpose.
    1.   To satisfy the obligation to a client to test any evidence being offered.
    2.   To develop facts favorable to the defense.
    3.   To discredit the witness.
    4.   To destroy the character of the witness, his/her story, or both.

B.   Facts favorable to the defense.
    1.   Eliciting a response from the investigator that suggests or acknowledges illegal behavior.
    2.   Show that there were others who had motive, were considered as suspects, and have not been ruled out.

C.   Discrediting the witness.
    1.   Bring out any latent evidence of bias or prejudice.
    2.   Test the memory of the witness to elicit contradictory or inconsistent statements.
    3.   Reveal that the direct testimony was unreasonable and questionable.
    4.   Show that the direct testimony was inaccurate, mistaken, or the result of an oversight.

D.   Destroying the witness's testimony.
    1.   Use of leading questions.
    2.   Use of rapid-fire questions.
    3.   Verbal brow-beating.
    4.   Intimidation, embarrassment.
    5.   Physical space encroachment.

E.   Objections—as to form and substance.
    1.   Form—when a question is unclear or confusing, improperly phrased, or argumentative.
    2.   Substance—relevancy, materiality, and competency of the question.
    3.   Alleged prior statements—prior written reports taken out of context.
    4.   Use of notes—defense attorney may examine notes.
    5.   Yes or no answers—may mislead, can ask judge to qualify and explain answer.
    6.   Timing of the response—should not answer too quickly in order to give time for the prosecutor to object.

Name: _____

QUIZ

1. The _____ has the burden of proof in a criminal trial.

2. Evidence given orally by a witness is known as _____ evidence.

3. Any tangible object or exhibit offered as proof is _____ evidence.

4. _____ evidence can be a chart, drawing, model, illustration, or experiment offered to the court to prove the truth or falsify the questions at issue.

5. In the _____ system, also known as the inquisitorial system, a person's guilt or innocence is decided by a judge.

6. The Anglican system is also known as the _____ system of justice.

7. _____ evidence, in itself, proves or refutes the fact at issue.

8. Evidence that provides indirect proof from which the fact at issue may be inferred is known as _____.

9. Attorneys may object as to _____ when a question is unclear or confusing, improperly phrased, or argumentative.

10. Evidence that is admissible under the rules of evidence for the purpose of proving a relevant fact is considered to be _____ evidence.

Name: _____

CROSSWORD PUZZLE

CLUES

Across

2. _____ evidence is indirect proof from which the fact at issue may be inferred.

5. _____ evidence can be a chart, drawing, model, illustration, or experiment.

9. _____ enables the defense to test evidence being offered, develop facts favorable to the defense, discredit the witness, or destroy the character of the witness or his/her testimony.

11. By itself, the _____ of evidence is not sufficient; it must also be material and competent.

13. An objection as to _____ is based on the relevancy, materiality, or competency of a question.

14. The legal system inherited from England and operative in the United States is the _____ system.

Down

1. An objection as to _____ is made when a question is unclear or confusing, improperly phrased, or argumentative.
3. Effective _____ is both understandable and believable.
4. _____ evidence, in itself, proves or refutes the fact at issue.
6. _____ is concerned with whether the evidence is sufficiently important to influence the outcome of the issue being contested.
7. _____ evidence is given orally by a witness.
8. _____ involves either the nature of the evidence itself or the person through whom it is offered in court.
10. A(n) _____ question is one that in its very asking supplies an answer.
12. _____ evidence is any tangible object or exhibit offered as proof.

Chapter 28
Putting It All Together:
The Assassination of Dr. Martin Luther King Jr.

LEARNING OBJECTIVES

1. Understand the usefulness of investigative strategy and practice in the criminal investigation process.
2. Identify and explain the investigative efforts used in the process of criminal investigation.
3. Compare and contrast the reactive behavior of investigators with the proactive behavior of investigators.
4. Describe the difference between crime pattern analysis and a targeted investigation.

KEY TERMS AND CONCEPTS

cold search
crime pattern analysis
investigative strategy
investigative tactics
proactive behavior
reactive behavior
targeted investigations

CHAPTER OUTLINE

I. The Investigation of the Assassination

    A.   U.S. Department of Justice Task Force review of FBI investigation.
        1. The murder occurred.
        2. Top-priority investigation ordered by FBI.
        3. Progress of the investigation.
            a.   Murkin files.
            b.   Informants and hate group activities checked.
            c.   Rooming house investigation.
            d.   Canipe Amusement Co.—evidence found.
            e.   Information and evidence tracked.
            f.   Memphis to Birmingham investigation shift.
            g.   Birmingham to Los Angeles shift.
            h.   Atlanta investigation.

        i.   Galt identified as James Earl Ray.

        j.   Passport search in Canada.

        k.   Ray apprehended in London, England.

  B.   Investigative summary.
    1. Crime occurred in Memphis but spread to other cities.
    2. Interplay between physical evidence, people, government files, and records.

II. Analysis of Investigative Efforts

  A.   The identification of a latent fingerprint.
    1. No computerized searches available during this time.
    2. Some 7,000 fingerprint cards had been examined until Ray's was located.

  B.   The number of unproductive and false leads.
    1. Leads from tips leading to unproductive efforts.
    2. Canvassing performed in King murder was of national scope and virtually impossible for local law enforcement to accomplish with limited resources.

  C.   The investigative process in general.
    1. People.
    2. Physical evidence.
    3. Records.

  D.   Activities if or when a potential suspect materializes.
    1. Review all reports and information on crime.
    2. Examine the arrest record, if any, on the suspect.
    3. Interview officers who have arrested the offender previously.
    4. Contact any custodial officers who may have gotten to know the suspect while s/he was incarcerated.
    5. Question the suspect.

III. Proactive Measures

  A.   Reactive behavior—investigating a crime after it has been committed.

  B.   Proactive behavior—anticipatory measures (i.e., banks with marked money and serial numbers recorded for robbery purposes).
    1. Crime pattern analysis—begins with analysis of reported crimes.
    2. Targeted investigation—focuses on the small group of career criminals responsible for an unduly large amount of crime.

Name: _____

QUIZ

1. _____ is the term used to describe the overall planning of operations in a criminal investigation.

2. _____ is the term used to describe the means employed to secure any designated objective in a criminal investigation.

3. The reason the FBI was called in to investigate the murder of Dr. King rather than the Memphis Police was _____.

4. _____ is an anticipatory crime-solution approach that focuses on a small group of career criminals responsible for a large amount of specific criminal activity.

5. _____ is a method to solve a series of crimes through measures taken in the expectation of having law enforcement ready for the next event.

6. _____ is used in anticipation of the commission of a crime, in order to prevent the crime from occurring, rather than after the fact.

7. An after-the-fact investigation of a crime is referred to as _____.

8. The central objective in every criminal investigation is to identify the offender and _____.

9. James Earl Ray was apprehended in the city of _____.

10. The systematic examination of fingerprint cards and comparison with latent prints without the use of computerized search methods is referred to as a(n) _____.

Chapter 29

Raids: Reflections on Their Management

LEARNING OBJECTIVES

1. Describe the issues, circumstances, and outcome of the Waco, Texas, incident involving the Branch Davidians.
2. Describe the issues, circumstances, and outcome of the Philadelphia, Pennsylvania, incident involving MOVE.
3. Describe the issues, circumstances, and outcome of the Chicago, Illinois, incident involving the Black Panther Party.
4. Identify the planning and staging considerations involved in the accomplishment of a raid.

KEY TERMS AND CONCEPTS

back-up equipment
Black Panther Party
Branch Davidian
communications systems
coordination
MOVE
personnel
raid
weaponry

CHAPTER OUTLINE

I. Introduction

A   Planning and staging of a raid requires five things:
1. Personnel.
2. Communications system.
3. Appropriate weaponry.
4. Back-up equipment (i.e., ambulances, fire engines).
5. Coordination.

B.   Guidance by looking at examples of raids.

II. Waco: The Branch Davidians

A.   Background.
1. Religious cult.

2. Involved in illegal weapons and explosives.
3. BATF raid to search for illegal weapons and explosives.

B. Criticisms.
1. Poor planning.
2. FBI tactics.
3. Failure to heed religious warnings given by Koresh.

III. Philadelphia: MOVE

A. Background.
1. Black separatist group with violent characteristics.
2. Local police involved.

B. Criticisms.
1. Bomb used to open a hole in a roof to drop tear gas.
2. Entire neighborhood destroyed by fire.
3. Poor planning.

IV. Chicago: The Black Panthers

A. Background.
1. Local officers searching for illegal weapons.
2. Gunfight resulting in two Panthers killed, four wounded; two officers with minor injuries.

B. Criticisms.
1. Two different stories told: one by police, the other by Panthers.
2. Grand jury problems in determining the facts.
3. Questions: Who polices the police? Who will judge the judges?

V. Summary

A. Perils inherent in this law enforcement activity—criticisms.

B. Learning from mistakes made.

C. Key to success.
1. Anticipation.
2. Planning.
3. Preparation.

Name: _____

QUIZ

1. According to the text, the planning and staging of a raid requires personnel, communications systems, appropriate weaponry, backup equipment, and _____.

2. The raid described in the text that involved the Bureau of Alcohol, Tobacco, Firearms, and Explosives was the raid of _____.

3. The standoff between the Branch Davidians and the ATF in Waco lasted _____ (how many?) days.

4. The MOVE and Black Panther incidents involved local police agencies, while the Branch Davidian raid involved the FBI and the _____.

5. The raids involving the Branch Davidians, MOVE, and the Black Panthers involved an initial search and seizure of _____.

6. The _____ incident was the result of a bomb dropped on a roof to open a hole for tear gas.

7. David Koresh read and taught predominately from the Book of _____ in the Bible.

8. According to the text, the key to success in a raid is to have anticipation, planning, and _____.

9. More than _____ people died in the Branch Davidian standoff.

10. The bomb dropped by police on the MOVE residence created a _____ that destroyed an entire neighborhood.

Chapter 30
Miscarriages of Justice

Learning Objectives

1. Understand the role each component of the criminal justice systems plays in contributing to miscarriages of justice.
2. Provide a definition of the term "miscarriage of justice."
3. Explain how the police and prosecution contribute to miscarriages of justice by helping to convict innocent defendants.
4. Explain how defense attorneys and judges contribute to miscarriages of justice through poor representation and improper trial procedures.
5. Explain how crime laboratories and expert witnesses contribute to miscarriages of justice through unethical practices and perjury.
6. Provide suggestions on how miscarriages of justice can be prevented.

Key Terms and Concepts

Capital Litigation Trial Bar (CLTB)
contract attorneys
exculpatory evidence
false confessions
harmless error
Innocence Project
pro bono
"testilying" and perjury

Chapter Outline

I. Introduction

A   Definition of miscarriage of justice.
1. Generally the term has been applied only to capital cases in which the defendant was found not guilty.
2. Definition is extended to include not only cases in which there was no conviction but to those that remain unsolved.

B.   High-profile cases.
1. The Nicole Brown Simpson/Ronald Goldman case is an example of a case in which the defendant was found not guilty.
2. The Jon Benet Ramsey case is an example of a case that remains unsolved.

II.   Police Misconduct

A.   Obtaining false confessions.
1.   To advance careers.
2.   Regularly obtained from those who are young, have low IQs or poor language skills, or have been abused or coerced.

B.   Other forms of police misconduct.
1.   Warrantless searches without probable cause.
2.   Coverups.
3.   Obtaining false statements from witnesses.
4.   Ignoring exculpatory evidence.
5.   Perjury in court.
6.   Improper lineup procedures.

III.   Prosecutor Misconduct

A.   Reasons for prosecutors to overstep legally accepted boundaries.
1.   To advance political careers.
2.   Prosecutors "graded" on number of convictions made.

B.   Methods used by unethical prosecutors.
1.   Leaking information to public.
2.   Withholding evidence from defense.
3.   Improper arguments made before a jury.
4.   Misleading the judge and/or jury.
5.   Paying witnesses to testify.

IV.   Defense Counsel Misconduct

A.   Reasons for misconduct.
1.   Improperly trained or experienced in criminal defense cases.
2.   Not taking enough time due to low payment for services.

B.   Method of misconduct.
1.   Failing to negotiate plea bargains.
2.   Failing to check out witness statements.
3.   Failing to properly prepare for trial.
4.   Failing to file motions and appeals in a timely manner.

V.   Judge Misconduct

A.   Reasons for misconduct.
1.   Eagerness to clear docket and have cases disposed of quickly.
2.   Personal biases and prejudices.

    B.   Methods of misconduct.
        1.   Allowing improper testimony to be heard by jury.
        2.   Improper jury selection process.
        3.   Refusing requests by defense to have access to forensic services.
        4.   Legal errors during trial.
        5.   Improper instructions provided to jurors.

VI. Contributions to Miscarriages of Justice by the Supreme Court

    A.   Reasons for contributing to miscarriages of justice.
        1.   Refusing to review cases due to "harmless error."
        2.   Allowing guilty verdicts to stand even though defendant was ineffectively represented by counsel.

    B.   Finality in decision is of greater importance than relief for the individual.
        1.   The belief is one of law rather than of what is just.
        2.   English courts have same views as U.S. courts in this matter.

VII. Suggestions for Improving the System

    A.   Police.
        1.   Use videotapes of confessions and lineups.
        2.   Verify eyewitness testimony and statements.
        3.   Censure and discipline police misconduct.

    B.   Attorneys.
        1.   Scrutinize inmate witnesses and paid witnesses.
        2.   Provide proper discovery of evidence.
        3.   Monitor use of low-paid attorneys.
        4.   Require minimum standards (CLTB) for capital case attorneys.

    C.   Legal process.
        1.   Censure and discipline misconduct by judges and attorneys.
        2.   Allow after conviction claims of innocence to be heard if new evidence is forthcoming.
        3.   Establish Innocence Projects.
        4.   Allow defense same access to forensic services as prosecution.

Name: _____

Quiz

1. Miscarriages of justice refers to guilty parties who were found not guilty and to cases that are _____.

2. Illicit police behavior transpires in many ways, but according to the text, _____ are the most troublesome.

3. In Illinois and _____, more death row inmates were exonerated than executed in the twentieth century.

4. One police misdeed is that _____ is substituted for investigation.

5. Prosecutors may sometimes use known liars or _____ to testify that a defendant confessed.

6. Indigent defendants run the risk of _____ representation from contract attorneys or court-appointed attorneys.

7. Judges may sometimes allow _____ evidence to be admitted, contributing to the miscarriage of justice.

8. The Supreme Court may express the belief that _____ is of greater importance than relief for the individual.

9. Forensic experts generally work for the prosecution and, consequently, _____ is sometimes (wrongly) regarded as their job.

10. Until the advancement of _____, it was usually difficult to prove a contention of innocence.

Name: _____

CROSSWORD PUZZLE

CLUES

Across

3. Attorneys who provide the lowest bid to represent indigent defendants.
5. Legal term explaining why a Supreme Court refuses to review cases with minor procedural barriers.
6. Minimum standards for counsel representing defendants in capital cases.
8. A word describing evidence that may exonerate a defendant.
9. Imprisoned in London for possessing explosives and had their convictions overturned in 1991.
10. Slang term for perjury.

Down

1. Regularly obtained from those who are young or have low IQs or poor language skills.

2. Provides legal representation and investigative assistance to convicts who claim to be innocent.

4. More death row inmates were exonerated than executed in Florida and _____ during the twentieth century.

7. According to the text, police depend too much upon _____ to seal the fate of the defendant and to advance their careers.

Exercises

Name: _____

Exercise 1

Crime Scene Sketch

Using one room of your home, draw a crime scene sketch. The "scene" should be a murder scene. Include in your sketch the following items required in all crime scene sketches:

1. North indication.
2. Legend showing what symbols mean, if not commonly known.
3. Case name, date, time; your name.
4. Location of "scene."
5. Measurements (coordinate for indoor scenes).
6. Evidentiary items (i.e., body, weapons, blood spatters, bullet holes, etc.).
7. Scale, if drawn to scale.

Use a cross-projection method. All objects are drawn as if seen from above, but the walls and ceiling are folded down and the items are drawn as if the room was a cardboard box with its sides flattened.

Complete a "rough" sketch and a finished sketch. You may make the finished sketch by hand or use a computer program.

Name: _____

Exercise 2

Death by Gunshot

You are a criminal investigator for a medium-sized police department. On Saturday, August 12 at 2:15 in the afternoon, you receive a call regarding a shooting at a residence. Upon arrival at the scene, you find two police patrol cruisers and one officer standing at the front door. There is also an ambulance with two attendants standing outside. You approach the officer.

"Hi Jim, what we got here?," you ask.

"Looks like a robbery/homicide. We've got one dead guy downstairs and the place looks like it's been ransacked. The medical guys here checked the body and confirmed that he was dead. I've notified the Coroner, too, but he hasn't gotten here yet," the officer responds.

"Who found the body?," you ask.

"This guy's wife. She and the two kids were out shopping and said he was OK when they left about 10:00 this morning. They're pretty distraught. They're in the living room with Officer Banks now."

"What's the name of the deceased?, " you ask.

"Jim McCain," the officer responds.

You enter the house and proceed to the living room, where you find the deceased's wife, Ms. McCain, and two children along with Officer Banks.

"Hello, I'm Detective Johnson. Are you Ms. McCain?

"Yes," Ms. McCain sobs.

"I know this is difficult for you right now but I need to get some information if I could. You feel up to it right now?," you ask.

"I guess," she responds.

"Is there anyone I can call for you to be here with you?," you ask.

"Maybe my Pastor, John Harrod," she says.

After getting Officer Banks to try to locate Pastor Harrod, you proceed to obtain as much information as you can from Ms. McCain, keeping in mind her emotional state. She is able to tell you that her husband was alive and well when she and the kids left shopping. There had been no arguments and her husband seemed to be in good spirits. She does not know of anyone that could have done this. She says the whole episode is a complete shock.

You go downstairs to the scene and find a partially open door to a finished basement den. The den has a stand-alone bookshelf unit that appears to have been ransacked. The den is carpeted with wood paneling on the walls. There are two windows and one exterior door. The door and windows are locked. The ceiling is suspended consisting, of 2 x 4 foot panels on metal suspension frames. There are four flush-mounted fluorescent light fixtures. There is a television on a stand, a couch, two easy chairs, and a desk. There is another chair out of place, turned on end in the middle of the floor. Near the chair is the body of Mr. McCain. There appears to be a single gunshot wound to the frontal portion of his head. Based on the powder stippling, it appears to be a close wound. There is no firearm present. However, there is an empty .25-caliber shell casing near the body. Mr. McCain's hands and feet are not bound. He is in a face-up position. The medical personnel at the scene inform you that he was found on his side and that they turned the body to a full face-up position to check vital signs.

After notifying crime scene search technicians for assistance, you ask Ms. McCain some additional questions. She informs you that the den was the only place that looked like it had been ransacked. The doors and windows of the house were intact and not broken. Ms. McCain says the only thing missing from the house is a safe box measuring about 9 x 12 inches. The box contained about $200 in cash, along with some insurance papers, a house deed, and other papers. She mentions that the robbers took the cash and the box but left the papers on the desk downstairs.

You notice a pile of papers neatly stacked on the desk in the downstairs den. There are a number of life insurance policies, a deed to the house, birth certificates for the children, a bank savings account book, and two certificates of deposit. These were the papers that were in the missing box. One of the crime scene technicians casually informs you that at least the wife and kids will be well taken care of from the amount of life insurance Mr. McCain had. You glance at the policies and note that they total to well over one million dollars. You immediately get a feeling that a suspect in this case might well be Ms. McCain.

"Detective, could I have a word with you?," asks Pastor Harrod, coming down the steps into the den.

"Be careful where you step, Pastor, we've not finished with processing the scene yet," you warn.

"Yes, I will. I just wanted to say how terrible I feel about this. Mr. McCain has been through so much pain and anguish the past few months I can't help but think this is God's way of relieving him."

"What do you mean?," you ask.

"He came to me two months ago for counseling. He didn't want his wife or children to know, so I never spoke with them about it. To my knowledge, they still don't know."

"Know what?," you ask impatiently.

"I thought you might have known. Mr. McCain had cancer. It was terminal, I understand," Pastor Harrod comments.

Another feeling comes over you. Could Mr. McCain have committed suicide? But where's the gun and the money box? A search of the house, vehicles, and area have turned up nothing. Neighbors neither heard nor saw anything. Ms. McCain's two young children confirm what she told you. You need more information.

Based on what you have read, answer the following questions.

1. Is the detective performing his job in the correct manner? Why or why not?
2. What physical evidence would you look for and where?
3. What persons would you want to interview for additional information and why?
4. What medical information would you want from the forensic pathologist?
5. What additional information would you be able to obtain by searching the crime scene again?
6. What do you think happened?

Name: _____

Exercise 3

Solvability Factors

You are a Lieutenant in the Criminal Investigation Division. Your responsibilities include assigning cases to three detectives under your command, case screening, and prioritizing cases to be worked. Below is a list of five cases. Prioritize these cases from 1 (highest priority) to 5 (lowest priority) based on type of offense and solvability factors. Next, estimate the amount of time each case will take or eliminate it from the workload. Assign cases to the three detectives as Detective One, Detective Two, and Detective Three. After prioritizing and assigning these cases, explain why you ranked and assigned them as you did. Discuss the investigative leads that are present in each case and what direction detectives should go in solving the cases. In addition, identify any outside agencies that may be of assistance to the investigation.

Case 1
Aggravated Rape. Victim: 22-year-old college student. Crime reported by victim's parents two days after the assault. Victim is generally uncooperative. No physical evidence. Victim most likely is acquainted with perpetrator but has not named the suspect. No known witnesses.

Rank: _____
Pursue as investigation: ____yes ____no
Detective assigned (if pursued): _____
Discussion:

Case 2
Burglary. Residence broken into. Only items of value stolen, namely firearms and electronics. No latent prints or trace evidence found. Victim has list of items stolen with serial numbers. Neighbor reports seeing a vehicle that matches the description of a vehicle seen at three other burglaries within the past two months. Partial tag number.

Rank: _____
Pursue as investigation: ____yes ____no
Detective assigned (if pursued): _____
Discussion:

Case 3

Larceny. Employee theft of merchandise. Retail store reports theft of more than $5,000 of merchandise from warehouse. Suspects limited to six employees. Stolen items are traceable through serial numbers. No physical evidence.

Rank: _____

Pursue as investigation: ____yes ____no

Detective assigned (if pursued): _____

Discussion:

Case 4

Child Abuse. Victim is six-year-old female. Routine school immunization and examination by pediatrician results in suspicion of child abuse. Unexplained bruising, scarring, and burn marks on victim. Upon questioning by pediatrician, parents became very agitated, upset, and defensive. Took victim home. Initial investigation by uniformed division found several neighbors who have witnessed severe physical discipline of the child by parents. Some witnesses fear for the safety of the child.

Rank: _____
Pursue as investigation: _____yes _____no
Detective assigned (if pursued): _____
Discussion:

Case 5

Homicide. Male victim found stabbed to death with 140 stab wounds in face, neck, and chest. Two witnesses can provide fairly good description of assailant. Most likely able to pick suspect out of a lineup. Victim known to frequent homosexual bars and clubs. No latent prints found on knife. No other trace evidence found.

Rank: _____
Pursue as investigation: _____ yes _____no
Detective assigned (if pursued): _____
Discussion:

Name: _____

Exercise 4

The Round-Up

You are a state criminal investigator reviewing the actions of a local police department's raid activities. During a police drug "roundup," two people were killed by police gunfire. Acting on closed indictments for drug dealers in the area, police spent the better part of the night making raids on various locations. During one of these raids, police entered a residence and surprised four people in one room where a computer was kept. One of the people picked up a shotgun and police officers fired, killing him and fatally wounding another person standing nearby. You have been requested by the District Attorney to make an investigation and report your findings to the Grand Jury. There has been much criticism of the police in the news media regarding this incident.

"OK, Officer Smith, you want to tell me what happened?," you ask.

"Not much to tell that I haven't already told a hundred times. We broke into the residence and heard noises coming from downstairs. We rushed down and found four people in one room. One of them picked up a shotgun and pointed it at me and I instinctively fired five times. Unfortunately, one of the bystanders was nearby and moved or something while I fired and one of my rounds hit them. It was an accident. Everything happened so quickly," Officer Smith replies.

You question the other officers that were at the scene and, for the most part, they confirmed the officer's story. However, one officer explains that he didn't see the incident but heard the shots ring out.

"Yeah, I was coming down the steps behind the other officers and I heard one blast from the shotgun and then Smith fired off his rounds," Officer Peebles states.

"No, I think Smith fired when that dude swung his shotgun toward him. When he got hit by Smith's bullets, his shotgun went off," Officer Jackson states.

You also interview witnesses at the scene, both of whom have the same story.

"We thought you guys were coming after the computer. Bill (deceased) had this child pornography thing going on you know. He was distributing child porno over the Internet. He always said if the cops came he was going to put a hole in his hard drive so they couldn't get nothing on him. When you guys came, he grabbed that shotgun and shot the computer CPU. Blew it all to pieces. Then that cop started shooting everywhere. I dove down behind the couch."

The physical evidence is undeniable. Bill, the first deceased, was shot three times in the chest and neck area. Adam, the bystander was shot once in the chest. A fourth round, from a .40-caliber Glock pistol, was found lodged in the wall. Five empty .40-caliber shell casings were found at the scene. The shotgun Bill used was a single-shot .410-gauge shotgun. One empty shell remained in the breech. The only shot pellets recovered were from a computer CPU. Shot distance analysis determined that the shotgun was almost in contact with the CPU at the hard drive location.

Record checks indicated that Bill, the deceased, had an arrest record for selling drugs, possession of narcotics, and child molestation. He was on the sex offender registry for the state. He had no known record for violence. His parole officer indicated that he was a passive, almost timid, individual and was surprised that he would resort to firing on a police officer.

You question Officer Smith further.

"No way. He pulled that shotgun at me. I fired and he went down. As he was going down, his shotgun discharged toward the computer," Smith maintains.

Based on what you have read, answer the following questions:

1.   How could this have been prevented in the first place? What steps would you have taken to ensure that arrests were made without people getting killed? What did the police do incorrectly?

2.   What evidence do you have to suggest Officer Smith is telling the truth? What evidence do you have to suggest the witnesses are telling the truth? What kinds of additional information would you need and where would you get it?